THE STORY OF
RUSSIA

R. VAN BERGEN, M. A.

1st WORLD
LIBRARY
Literary Society

The Story of Russia

R. Van Bergen

© 1st World Library, 2007
PO Box 2211
Fairfield, IA 52556
www.1stworldlibrary.com
First Edition

LCCN: 2007927850

Softcover ISBN: 978-1-4218-4565-4
Hardcover ISBN: 978-1-4218-4481-7
eBook ISBN: 978-1-4218-4649-1

Purchase *"The Story of Russia"*
as a traditional bound book at:
www.1stWorldLibrary.com/purchase.asp?ISBN=978-1-4218-4565-4

1st World Library is a literary, educational organization
dedicated to:

- Creating a free internet library of downloadable ebooks

- Hosting writing competitions and offering book publishing
scholarships.

Interested in more 1st World Library books? contact:
literacy@1stworldlibrary.com
Check us out at: www.1stworldlibrary.com

1st World Library Literary Society

Giving Back to the World

"If you want to work on the core problem, it's early school literacy."

- James Barksdale, former CEO of Netscape

"No skill is more crucial to the future of a child, or to a democratic and prosperous society, than literacy."

- Los Angeles Times

"Literacy... means far more than learning how to read and write... The aim is to transmit... knowledge and promote social participation."

- UNESCO

"Literacy is not a luxury, it is a right and a responsibility. If our world is to meet the challenges of the twenty-first century we must harness the energy and creativity of all our citizens."

- President Bill Clinton

"Parents should be encouraged to read to their children, and teachers should be equipped with all available techniques for teaching literacy, so the varying needs and capacities of individual kids can be taken into account."

- Hugh Mackay

To

HENRY MATHER LOWMAN

AMICUS CERTUS RE INCERTA CERNITUR.

CONTENTS

PREFACE

Recent events have drawn the attention upon Russia, a country of which but little is known here, because the intercourse between it and the United States has been limited. In my frequent journeys to the Far East, I found it often difficult to comprehend events because, while I could not help perceiving that the impulse leading to them came from Russia, it was impossible to discover what prompted the government of the czar. I felt the necessity to study the history of Russia, and found it so fascinating, that I resolved to place it in a condensed form before the students in our schools. They must be the judges of how I have succeeded.

R. VAN BERGEN.

I

THE REALM OF THE CZAR

When we think of our country, we feel proud of it for other and better reasons than its great size. We know how its extent compares with that of other nations; we know that the United States covers an area almost equal to that of Europe, and, more favored than that Grand Division, is situated on the two great highways of commerce, the Atlantic and Pacific Oceans. Europe is as far from the latter, as Asia is from the former; and these highways, powerful means toward creating prosperity, remain at the same time barriers whereby nations that find greater delight in the arts of war than in those of peace, are restrained from disturbing our national progress.

At the beginning of this twentieth century the nations upon which depends the world's peace or war, happiness or misfortune, are the United States, Great Britain, Germany, France, Austria-Hungary, Italy, Russia, Japan, and in the near future China. Here we see that Europe, although little larger in area than the United States, is represented by seven nations, Asia by two, and the Western Hemisphere by one which by its institutions stands for peace and progress, for law and order. Hence we, its citizens, are known all over the world as Americans.

If we compare the area occupied by the several European powers with that covered by the main body of our republic, that is, not including Alaska and other outlying territories, we find that Austria-Hungary has four thousand square miles less than Texas, while Germany lacks forty thousand square miles in comparison with the Lone Star State. France is four thousand square miles less than Germany, and Italy is only a thousand square miles greater than Nevada. The British Kingdom in Europe is about twice the area of Illinois. Among the great nations of the world, aside from outlying possessions beyond the Grand Division, our country stands third, and should occupy the second place, because China, the next larger, owes its greater area to territories over which she has little or no control, and which she seems destined to lose.

The largest country is Russia, covering as it does one-sixth of all the land on the earth. This empire, although inhabited by people differing in race, religion, and customs, is one compact whole. It embraces in Europe 2,113,000 square miles, or more than all other European nations combined; its area in Asia is 6,672,000 square miles, making a total of 8,785,000 square miles, or 2.8 times as many as the main body of our country. All the people living in this immense empire, whatever their race, religion, or language, obey the will of *one man*. We, who dwell in our beloved country, yield obedience only to the Law; but the laws are made by ourselves, and they allow us to do as we please, so long as we do not interfere with others who have the same rights; and those laws are ever ready to protect us. In Russia laws are made or unmade at the will of one person who is himself above the laws. Every man, woman, or child, born and living in that country, is at his mercy. Mere suspicion is sufficient to drag a man from his family and home, perhaps to disappear without leaving a trace. Such a government is called an autocracy, and the man who may thus dispose of people's life and property, is known as an Autocrat. Hence the title of the Emperor of Russia is: Autocrat of All the Russias.

Why "All the Russias"? Look at the map of Eurasia, the continent embracing the two Grand Divisions Europe and Asia. You will see that the Russian Empire is bounded on the north by the Arctic Ocean; on the east by the Bering Strait, the Bering Sea, the Sea of Okhotsk, and the Japan Sea; on the south by China, Pamir, Afghanistan, Persia, Asiatic Turkey, and the Black Sea; and on the west by Roumania, Austria-Hungary, the German Empire, the Baltic Sea, Sweden, and Norway. This immense empire is the growth of many centuries, and even in Europe it has not yet been welded into one whole. When we read Russian books, we learn about Great and Little Russia, White and Red Russia, which shows that divisions of bygone years are still observed by the people. Much has been done towards effacing those boundary lines; but the fact that the czar, autocrat though he is, recognizes and admits the division in his title, shows that even he is, to some extent, subject to public opinion.

Russia in Europe, however, with the exception of Poland and Finland, is a country with one religion and one language; that is, the czar and his government recognize and admit no other. That is the cause of the persecution of the Jews, four fifths of whom dwell in the southwest of Russia in an area covering 356,681 square miles, which is sometimes mentioned as the Jewish territory. Every succeeding czar has tried to make all his subjects think and act in the manner prescribed by him. The process is known as "Russianizing," and goes on incessantly in its different stages. Immediately after the conquest of a country, its people are assured that their religion, institutions, and language, shall be respected; the only difference is that the native officials are displaced by Russians. This continues until Russian rule is firmly established, and no one dreams of resisting the czar. Then the Russian language displaces the native tongue, and if disturbances occur, the military is called in to inflict a terrible punishment. The loss of the native language carries with it that of old institutions, and when the people have submitted to their fate, it is the turn of their religion. The Russian is in no hurry; he has a conviction that time has no changes in store for his empire, hence he bides his time, and is likely to succeed in his purpose. This process is now carried on in Central Asia where Russian power has found its greatest expansion in modern times. It is but fair to admit that Russian absorption there has been highly beneficial because robber tribes were reduced to law and order.

Before telling the Story of Russia, that is, of how the huge empire was formed and grew to its present size, it is necessary to become better acquainted with the aspect and nature of the country. Looking at the map of the Eurasian continent, that is, the continent embracing Europe and Asia, we cannot fail to notice that Russia is a country of the plains. Its southern boundary seems to follow the mountain barriers which divide Asia into two parts. Does it not seem as if long billows of earth roll down toward the Arctic Ocean, where they rest benumbed by the eternal cold? These mountains branch off toward the south, east or west, but scorn to throw so much as a spur northward. It is true that a solitary chain, the Urals, runs north and south, but it stands by itself, and is nothing more than what the word Ural signifies, a *belt* or *girdle* separating the European from his Asiatic brother. These mountains do not form the backbone of a country, nor do they serve as a watershed, like our Rocky Mountains or the Andes of South America. Some of their peaks rise to a height of 6,000 feet above the level of the sea, but the chain, 1531 miles long, seems destined only to keep the two races apart.

R. Van Bergen

Beyond the Ural mountains, the plain resumes its sway. This extensive flat could not fail to exert a noticeable influence upon the country and its inhabitants. The dense forests in the north, while acting as a screen, do not afford protection against the icy polar winds which sweep with scarcely diminished force over the broad expanse, so that the northern shores of the Black and Caspian Seas in January have about the same temperature as Stockholm, the capital of Sweden. The mountains of Western Europe shut off the aerial current of the Gulf Stream which tempers the summer heat as well as the winter cold. Russia's climate, therefore, is one of extremes. In summer the heat is very oppressive, owing to the absence of the sea breeze which elsewhere affords so much relief; and when a wind does blow, it only adds to the discomfort, because it has lost its moisture. That is the reason why Russia suffers so often from drought. This is especially the case in the south where no forests are found to attract rain.

Nature has provided a substitute in the splendid waterways. In about the center of European Russia, rises the Valdai plateau to a height of 1,100 feet above the sea level. This is Russia's great watershed. Near it, in Lake Volgo, rises the largest river of Europe, "Mother Volga," as the Russian ballad singers love to call it. Its entire length is 2,336 miles, or nearly the length of the Missouri; it has a basin of 590,000 square miles. Owing to the slight slope of the land, the great river flows placidly in its bed, which is fortunate since its Waters are swollen by several large rivers, so that there are points where it is seventeen miles wide. The Kama, one of the tributaries of the Volga, is 1,266 miles long; the Oka, another confluent, has a length of 633 miles. At Kazan, the Volga is 4,953 feet wide, at Jaroslaf 2,106 feet, and at Samara, 2,446 feet. It empties into the Caspian Sea, with a delta of more than seventy branches. The fish caught in this river often grow to gigantic proportions; its sturgeons, lampreys, and salmon, are highly prized. Since time immemorial, the Volga has been a great highway of trade. Kostroma, Nishni Novgorod, Kazan, Simbirsk, Saratof, and Astrakhan, are the most populous cities on its banks.

Other large rivers rise on the Valdai plateau. The Dnieper runs south, passing by Kief, and empties in the Black Sea, near Odessa. The Dwina runs northward, seeking the icy Arctic, which it enters by way of the White Sea near Archangel. The Duena takes a westerly course towards the Gulf of Riga where it empties near the city of that name. Of greater importance are the small streams which feed Lakes Ladoga and Onega, because they connect Central Russia with the Baltic Sea by means of the Neva.

European Russia is usually divided into four zones or belts, from the character of the soil and the nature of its productions; their general direction is from southwest to northeast. In the north, as a screen against the Arctic blast, is the *poliessa* or forest region, densely covered with lindens, birches, larches, and sycamores, with oaks on the southern fringe. These forests are invaluable to Russia where, in the absence of mountains, stone is scarce. The houses are built of wood, and fires are of common occurrence. Both lumber and fuel are supplied by these forests which originally extended to Novgorod, Moscow, and Jaroslaf. The increase in population together with the growing demand for lumber, have caused extensive clearings; but the area covered by the forests is so large, that the supply is well-nigh inexhaustible.

South of this zone are the black earth lands, extending down to the Caucasus and across the Urals, and covering in Europe an area of one hundred and fifty million acres,—equal to that of Texas. This zone derives its name from an apparently inexhaustible bed of black mold, so rich that no manure is required to produce abundant crops. Until late in the last

R. Van Bergen

century, and before the United States began to export its surplus harvests, this region was considered the granary of Europe. It was known in very old times since we read of it in the Heroic Age of Ancient Greece, when Jason sailed in the Argo to bring home the Golden Fleece.

Almost equal in extent is the zone of arable steppes, or prairies, once the home of the Cossack, the nomad who led here the life of a shepherd king, moving about as the condition of pasture and flock required. Most of this land is now under cultivation, and with careful farming produces good crops. These arable steppes cover an area equal to that of Iowa, Kansas, and Nebraska.

The fourth and last zone is that of the barren steppes. There is ample evidence that at some remote time these plains were covered with salt water. The Caspian Sea has a level eighty feet below that of the Black Sea, and it is therefore probable that here was a large inland sea of which the Caspian and Aral Seas are the remains. These steppes are unfit for farming. Here dwell the Kalmucks and Kirghizes, descendants of the Tartars whose yoke once pressed heavily upon Russia.

II

EARLY RECORDS OF RUSSIA

At an early period in the history of Greece, we hear of colonies established on the northern shore of the Pontus Euxinus or Hospitable Sea, as they named the Black Sea. We may even now recognize some of the names of those colonies, such as Odessos, at the mouth of the Bug, Tyras, at that of the Dniester, and Pityas where Colchis, the object of the search of Jason and his fellow Argonauts, is supposed to have been. In the fourth century before our era, some of these colonies united under a hereditary *archon* or governor, probably for the purpose of securing better protection against the barbarians who dwelt further inland.

The Greeks mention these barbarians as the Scythians, and divided them into three classes. The agricultural Scythians dwelt in the black earth belt, near the Dnieper; the nomad Scythians lived at some distance to the east of them, and the royal Scythians occupied the land around the Sea of Azof.

Learned men of Russia have made many excavations on the spots where the Greek settlements once stood, during the past century. They have been rewarded by finding many works of art, illustrating the mode of living of the Scythians. They have been placed, and may be seen in the Hermitage museum of St. Petersburg. Among these relics of the past are two beautifully engraved vases, one of gold, the other of silver. The Scythians on the silver vase wear long hair and beards, and are dressed in gowns or tunics, and bear a close resemblance to the Russians of our time. These vases and other ancient objects confirm what is said about these people by Herodotus, a Greek historian who lived in the fourth century before Christ.

We learn from him that the Scythians worshiped a sword stuck into the ground, representing the god of war, and that they made human sacrifices. They drank the blood of the first enemy killed in battle, scalped their prisoners, and used their skulls as drinking cups. In the course of time the Greek civilization exerted its influence, and penetrated to tribes dwelling much further in the north, as is shown by the antiquities found in the government of Ekaterinoslaf.

The *orbis terrarum* or world so far as it was known to the Greeks, was centered about the Mediterranean; hence the name of that sea, meaning Middle of the Land or Middle of the Earth. Beyond that there was an unknown region, supposed to be inhabited by people of whom many wonderful stories were told. Thus they believed in the existence of the Arimaspians, a race of one-eyed people; there are legends, too, of the Agrippei who were described as bald and snub-nosed. The Greeks also mention the Gryphons, who, they said, were guardians of immense quantities of gold. The most wonderful people to the Greeks were the Hyperboreans, or dwellers beyond the regions of the north wind, who were looked upon with awe and pity because it was said that they lived in a country where snow fell summer and winter. These were some of the races and tribes supposed to inhabit Russia, which goes far to prove that the knowledge of that country, in those times, was neither extensive nor very accurate.

The truth is that we know very little about the early inhabitants of Russia; nor do they concern us greatly, because grave changes occurred in the fourth century of our era. At that time several large and warlike tribes of Central Asia moved westward compelling other tribes on their route to join them or to move ahead. Thus they gathered strength until it looked as if Asia was bent upon the conquest of Europe. They poured in through the gap between the Ural mountains and the Caspian Sea, and the civilized people of southeastern Europe were unable to cope with the savage hordes. In the vanguard were the Goths, who made an effort to settle, in Scythia, but they were forced to move on when Attila, who is known as the Scourge of God, swooped down upon them with his Huns. He was followed by a host of Finns, Bulgarians, Magyars, and Slavs who, however, left his wake, scattered and settled down. Soon after the Slavs became known to Greek authors and were described by them. They were divided into a number of tribes, among them the Russian Slavs who settled about the sources of the Volga and the Oka, and were the founders of Novgorod, Pskof, and Izborsk.

They must have been a numerous people. We hear of another tribe settling on the banks of the Vistula, and laying the foundation of the future kingdom of Poland. They settled on the upper Elbe, and in the north of Germany. It is believed that the Slavs are ancestors of the people in Bohemia, Bulgaria, Croatia, Servia, and Dalmatia, and in Prussia of those living in Pomerania and Brandenburg.

All these Slavs, although widely dispersed, practiced the same heathen rites, spoke the same language, and nursed the same traditions, until they fell under different influences. They were, however, not the sole occupants of northeastern Europe. Other races had followed in Attila's wake, and among them the Finns were the most numerous and most warlike. They settled in the basin of the Dwina and the Kama and named their new home Biarmaland, while the Russians called it Great Permia. They also occupied what is now known as Finland, but which was then known as Land of the Suomi. The Finns, more than any other tribe, bore evidence of their Asiatic origin.

Thus the present European Russia was divided among a host of tribes, belonging either to the Slav or Finn families, and each kept to a great extent the superstitions and traditions of his race. Even in our time the traces of these superstitions are plainly discernible in many parts of Russia. When Christianity was introduced among these people, the missionaries found many of the barbaric rites so strongly implanted among the people that, instead of making vain efforts to uproot them, they preferred to admit them under a Christian name.

The religion of the Slavs bore a great resemblance to that of the Norsemen and of the Germanic races; that is, they worshiped nature and its phenomena. Dagh Bog was the sungod; Perun, the Thor of northern mythology, was the god of thunder; Stri Bog, the god of the winds; Voloss, the protector of flocks. They had neither temples nor regular priests, but worshiped the oak as the symbol of Perun, and before it the leaders offered sacrifices. These ancient deities are preserved under the names of St. John, who displaced Perun; Voloss who became St. Vlaise, etc. When a chief died, the wife often refused to survive her husband. The men-servants were summoned and asked which of them would be buried with his master. When one of them came forward, he was immediately strangled. Then the same question was put to the women servants, and if one of them consented, she was feasted until the day when the funeral pyre awaited the corpse. She was then killed and her body burned with that of her master. There were, however, some tribes that buried their dead.

The father was absolute master of his family, but his authority did not descend to the eldest son, but to the oldest of the family, his brothers, if any were living, according to their age. The Slavs kept several wives, and were given to consume large quantities of a strong drink called kvass. They were a people devoted to agriculture; the land under cultivation was not owned by one person or a family, but by all the members of a community, or *mir*. The heads of the families composing the mir assembled in a council or *vetche*, which had authority over the mir. Only the house and the *dvor* or inclosure, and his share in the harvest, were the property of each householder. In the course of time, several of these rural communities united in a canton or county, called a *volost*, which was then governed by a council composed of the elders of several communes. It happened sometimes that one of these elders, who was considered unusually wise or powerful, became chief of the volost, a dignity which might become hereditary. This was probably the origin of the boyards or nobles. As a rule, the volosts were proud of their independence; they disliked entangling alliances, although in time of danger or necessity they would enter into a confederacy of all the counties belonging to the same tribe, which was then called *plemia*. But it was always understood that such an arrangement was temporary. In most of the volosts, there was at least one spot fortified by earthen walls and wooden palisades, where the people might take refuge in case of an attack.

We know that some of the Slav tribes attained some degree of civilization as early as the seventh century of our era. Novgorod was a town, large for that time, which carried on a brisk trade with Asia. This is amply proved by the discovery of Asiatic coins belonging to that period. Although the favorite occupation of the Slavs was agriculture, the

R. Van Bergen

construction of the fortified places suggests that they were not averse to increase their wealth by an occasional raid upon their unprepared neighbors. There is other evidence that Novgorod, grown into a wealthy city in the middle of the ninth century, longed for peace. No wonder that such a community sought for means of security for its commerce. But the manner in which it accomplished this desire, decided the fate of Russia.

III

THE NORSEMEN (OR VARINGIANS) IN RUSSIA

It would have been strange indeed, if the bold Norsemen, the bold buccaneers who in their frail craft pillaged the west coasts of Europe and extended their voyages into the Mediterranean, should have omitted to pay a visit to the shores of the Baltic Sea. We know that they settled in England and France, and it causes no surprise when we read that the Slavs in the neighborhood of the Baltic paid tribute to them. They must have been exacting tax collectors, because we read also that, in 859, the Slavs rose and expelled their visitors. Three years later they returned at the invitation of the people of Novgorod. .

Nestor, the historian of the Slav race, who lived in the twelfth century, and whose account is remarkably clear and trustworthy, wrote that the inhabitants of Novgorod "said to the princes of Varingia, 'Our land is great and fertile, but it lacks order and justice; come, take possession, and govern us.'"

The invitation was accepted. Three brothers, Rurik or the Peaceful, Sineous or the Victorious, and Truvor or the Faithful, proceeded to Russia with their families and fighting men. Rurik settled on the south shore of Lake Ladoga,

Sineous on the White Lake, and Truvor at Izborsk. The two younger brothers died, and Rurik moved to Novgorod where he built a castle. At about the same time two other Norsemen, Askold and Dir, landed in Russia, and went to Kief, then also a flourishing city, where they were equally well received. They persuaded its people to prepare an expedition against Czargrad, the City of the Czar or Emperor of the Eastern Roman Empire, now known as Constantinople, but at that time named Byzantium. The expedition of Kief under Askold and Dir sailed down the Dnieper in a fleet of 200 large boats, entered the Golden Horn—or Bosphorus,—and began the siege of Constantinople. The capital was saved by the Patriarch or head of the Greek Church, who plunged a wonder-working robe into the waves, whereupon a violent storm destroyed the Russian fleet.

The two chiefs, Askold and Dir, must have escaped, because they were back at Kief when that city received a disagreeable visit. Upon Rurik's death, he was succeeded, not by his son Igor, but by his brother Oleg as the eldest of the family. The new prince or *kniaz* did not approve of rival Norsemen in his neighborhood. With his own men and a large number of Slavs and Finns, he marched upon Kief, and on his way compelled Smolensk and Loubetch to submit to his authority.

When he arrived before Kief, he succeeded in capturing Askold and Dir who were put to death "because," Oleg explained, "they were neither princes themselves, nor of the blood of princes." Kief was taken, and Oleg took up his residence in that city.

It is at this time that the name Russia first appears. Its derivation is doubtful and is, besides, of no great importance. Oleg ruled over Russia, that is, the plain extending from Kief to Novgorod. There is a story that he was defeated by the

Hungarians, who had crossed the Dnieper, but it is doubtful, because in the year 907, we find him preparing another expedition against Constantinople. On this occasion the people of that capital forgot to bring out the robe, and tried to poison the invaders, but their scheme was discovered in time; they were forced to pay a heavy tribute and Oleg secured, besides, a very advantageous commercial treaty.

One of the wizards at Oleg's court had warned him that his favorite horse would be the cause of his death, and the animal was kept away from him until it died. Oleg did not believe in wizards; he insisted upon seeing the body and entered the stable. A snake came out of the horse's skull and stung Oleg in the foot, and he died from the effect of the poison.

Igor, Rurik's son, was the eldest, and succeeded his uncle. He led another expedition against Constantinople, but it ended in disaster, because the Russian fleet was destroyed by Greek fire. A large number of Russians were captured but Igor escaped. This failure did not prevent him from again attacking the Byzantine Empire, and this time he was successful. The emperor agreed to pay tribute and signed another commercial treaty.

Nestor, the Russian historian, tells us the story of Igor's death. "In the year 945," he says, "the *drujina*" (that is, the body-guard, composed of Norsemen or their descendants), "of Igor said to him, 'The men of Sveneld are richly provided with weapons and garments, while we go in rags; lead us, Prince, to collect the tribute so that thou and we may become rich.' Igor consented, and conducted them to the Drevlians to raise the tribute. He increased the first imposts, and did them violence, he and his men; after having taken all he wanted, he returned to his city. While on the road he bethought himself and said to his drujina, 'Go on with the tribute; I will go back and try to get some more out of them.' Leaving the greater part of his men to go on their way, he returned with only a few, to the end that he might increase his riches. The Drevlians, when they learnt that Igor was coming back, held council with Nal, their prince. 'When the wolf enters the sheepfold he slays the whole flock, if the shepherd does not slay him. Thus it is with us and Igor; if we do not destroy him, we are lost.' Then they sent deputies who said to him, 'why dost thou come anew unto us? Hast thou not collected all the tribute?' But Igor would not hear them, so the Drevlians came out of the town of Korosthenes, and slew Igor and his men, for they were but a few."

The drujina or body-guard of the duke was at the same time his council. The men composing it were considered as members of his family; they ate at his table and shared his amusements as well as his toil. He did nothing without consulting them, and was really but the first among his peers. They formed a court of justice, and it was from among them that he appointed the voievods or governors of fortresses, and possadniks or commandants of large towns. We have a description of the courts of that time by an Arab writer named Ibn Dost. He says: "When a Russian brings a complaint against another, he summons him before the court of the prince where both state their case. When the prince has pronounced his verdict, his orders are executed; but if both parties are dissatisfied, the dispute must be decided by weapons. He whose sword cuts sharper, gains his cause. At the time of the fight, the relatives of the two adversaries appear armed, and surround the space set apart. The combatants then come to blows, and the victor may impose any terms he pleases."

The people of the country, the peasants, were not quite so free as when Rurik landed. They began to be known as *moujik*, a contemptuous diminutive of the word mouj or man, literally manikin. The merchants or *gosti* did not form a distinct class, but in larger cities, such as Novgorod and Kief, they had a voice in the administration. These cities had a vetche or municipal council which directed the city's business without any direct interference from the prince. The successors of Rurik attended to the defense of the country, the administration of justice, and the collection of tribute and taxes, which sources of revenue were appropriated by them and served for their support and for that of the drujina.

The Slavs of that time exhibited many characteristics which we recognize in the Russians of our time. Leo the Deacon, a noted writer of that time, mentions that they fought in a compact body, and seemed like a wall of iron, bristling with lances, glittering with shields, whence rang a ceaseless clamor like the waves of the sea. A huge shield covered them to their feet, and, when they fought in retreat, they turned this enormous buckler on their backs and became invulnerable. The fury of the battle frenzied them. They were never seen to surrender. When victory was lost they stabbed themselves, for they believed that those who died by the hand of an enemy were condemned to serve him in the life after death. The emperors of Byzantium were glad to secure their services, and the *ross*, as they called them, often formed the body-guard. In the Byzantine expedition against Crete, 700 Russians served in the army.

The Norsemen readily adapted themselves to the habits, customs, and language of the people among whom they settled. We find the Norse names of Rurik, Oleg, and Igor, but after the last named their descendants were Russians and bore Russian names.

At Igor's death his son Sviatoslaf was still a minor, whose mother, Olga, became Regent. She was a woman of determination, whose first thought was to avenge the death of her husband. The Drevlians, hearing of her preparations, sent two deputations to appease her: not a man returned. They were all put to death at her command. Nestor tells us that Olga herself commanded her warriors at the siege of Korosthenes, and that she offered to make peace on payment of a tribute of three pigeons and three sparrows for every house. This was accepted and the birds were delivered, when she ordered lighted tow to be fastened to their tails, and when they flew back to the wooden town, they set fire to the houses and barns. Korosthenes was then captured and a great number of its inhabitants were slaughtered and the rest were made slaves.

It seems strange that such a woman should have been the first of Rurik's house to embrace Christianity. There is no doubt that she visited Constantinople where she astonished the emperor by the force of her character. She was baptized and received the name of Helen. It is quite possible that she came to Constantinople for that purpose, because we read that she refused to be baptized at Kief "for fear of the pagans." This confirms the Greek records in which it is stated that a bishop was established in Russia, probably at Kief, in the time of Oleg.

It is not strange that Christianity should have taken root in Russia after the frequent wars with the Byzantine Empire, and considering the commerce carried on between Kief and Constantinople. Missionaries entered Russia at an early period. Two of them, Cyril and Methodius, prepared a Slavonic alphabet, in which many Greek letters were used, and the Bible was translated into that language. There is a tradition that Askold was baptized after his defeat at Constantinople, and that this is the reason why the people still worship at his tomb at Kief, as of that of the first Christian prince. The Norsemen had no taste for persecution on account of religious belief, but for themselves they clung to the heathen deities. When Igor swore to observe the treaty concluded with Emperor Leo VI, he went up to the hill of Perun and used the ancient Slavonic rites; but the emperor's deputies went to the church of St. Elias, and there laid their hands upon the Bible as a token of good faith.

The drujina and warriors did not take kindly to Christianity. They, as well as the peasants, preferred to worship Perun and Voloss. The same thing happened elsewhere. Christianity made the greatest progress in cities, whereas the dwellers on the "heath" remained "heathen." "When one of the warriors of the prince wished to become a convert," says Nestor, "he was not prevented; they simply laughed at him." When Olga returned from Constantinople, she was anxious that her son, who was of age and had succeeded to his father, should follow her example. Sviatoslaf refused; "my men will laugh at me," was his usual answer. Nestor mentions that he some-times lost his temper. Christianity did not make much progress during his reign.

He was a warrior, like his Norse ancestors. In the brief time of eight years, 964-972, he found time to wage two wars. The first was with the Khazar empire on the Don. Sviatoslaf captured its capital, the White City, and received tribute from two tribes of the Caucasus. The second war did not turn out so well.

From Nestor's account and that of Leo the Deacon, it appears that the Byzantine emperor, wishing to make use of Sviatoslaf, decided to find out what sort of man he was. He therefore sent him presents of gold and fine clothes, but the grandson of Rurik would scarcely look at them and told his warriors to take them away. When the emperor heard this, he sent him a fine sword and other weapons; these were accepted with every token of satisfaction by Sviatoslaf. When the emperor was informed of the result, he exclaimed:

R. Van Bergen

"This must be a fierce man, because he despises wealth and accepts a sword as tribute."

This did not prevent the emperor, who had a private quarrel with Peter, Czar of Bulgaria, from urging Sviatoslaf to make war upon his enemy. The Russian gave a hearty consent, and in a very short time he captured several fortresses and Pereiaslaf, the capital, fell into his hands. He determined to transfer his capital there, and when he returned to Kief, he told his mother of the city on the Danube. "The place," he said, "is the central point of my territory, and abounds in wealth. Precious goods, gold, wine, and all kinds of fruit, come from Greece. Silver and horses are brought from the country of the Czechs and Hungarians, and the Russians bring money, furs, wax, and slaves."

Meanwhile the emperor of Constantinople was dead; his successor, John Zimisces was a very different man, who preferred having a weak Bulgarian ruler as his neighbor, instead of an empire which, even at that time, extended from Lakes Ladoga and Onega to the Balkans. He, therefore, made up his mind to oust the Russians. Sviatoslaf had left Bulgaria, but he returned and reconquered it, when he received a demand from the new emperor to execute the treaty entered into with his predecessor, that is, to leave Bulgaria. Sviatoslaf replied proudly that he expected to visit the emperor at Constantinople before long, but Zimisces, a brave and able man, took measures to prevent it. Before Sviatoslaf expected him, Zimisces attacked and defeated the Russians in the defiles of the Balkan, and soon after stormed and captured Pereiaslaf. Eight thousand Russians withdrew into the castle, which they defended heroically. They refused to surrender and, when the castle set on fire, they perished in the flames.

When Sviatoslaf heard of this disaster, he advanced against

the emperor. The Greek historian says that the Russian army was 60,000 men strong, but Nestor gives the number at 10,000. The two armies met and both fought with desperate valor, but at last the Russians gave way before the furious charges of the Greek cavalry—the Ironsides—and withdrew to Dorostol. Zimisces started in pursuit, and laid siege to the city where the same courage was displayed. After Sviatoslaf drew his men up out of the city and prepared to give battle, Zimisces proposed to him to decide the issue by a personal fight, but the offer was declined. "I know better than my enemy what I have to do," said Sviatoslaf. "If he is weary of life, there are a thousand ways by which he can end his days." The battle ended in defeat for the Russians who, Leo the Deacon tells us, left 15,500 dead, and 20,000 shields on the battlefield. Sviatoslaf was compelled to come to terms. Zimisces permitted him and what remained of his army to return to Russia, after he had sworn by Perun and Voloss that he would never again invade the empire, but would help in defending it against its enemies. If he broke his oath, he wished that he might "become as yellow as gold, and perish by his own arms." Zimisces showed the nobility of a brave man. He sent messengers to a warlike tribe requesting a free passage for the Russians; but this tribe was anxious to seize the opportunity. Sviatoslaf and his men were attacked near the Cataracts of the Dnieper; he was killed, but most of his men escaped. (A.D. 972.)

IV

SAINT VLADIMIR AND IAROSLAF THE GREAT

Sviatoslaf had divided the empire among his three sons; he left Novgorod to Vladimir, the eldest; Oleg, the second, was made prince of the Drevlians, and the youngest, Iaropolk, received Kief. As happens often, none of the three was satisfied with his share, and civil wars followed. Oleg was killed by Iaropolk, whereupon the youngest son of Sviatoslaf was slain by his brother Vladimir, who thus became the sole heir and successor to his father. His first act was to make war upon Poland. He compelled it to restore Red Russia or Old Gallicia, a territory in our time divided into seven governments, or provinces. He also reduced two revolted tribes, and forced the Lithuanians and Livonians to pay tribute.

At the beginning of his reign, Vladimir showed an unusual devotion to the old Slav gods. He erected idols on the sandy cliffs of Kief; that of Perun had a head of silver and a beard of gold. It seems that after some time he became displeased with this religion and, Nestor tells us, he grew anxious to know what religion was the best. He, therefore, sent deputies to Bulgaria to study the Moslem or Mohammedan creed, and to the Khazars, who occupied the plain between the Bug and the Volga, to make inquiries about the Jewish faith. From the Poles and Germans he wanted to know all about the

Roman Catholic Church, and at Constantinople he expected to learn of the Greek faith. When these deputies returned and reported to him, Vladimir selected the Greek Church, which choice was approved by his drujina; "if the Greek religion had not been the best, your grandmother Olga, the wisest of mortals, would not have adopted it," said they. Thus Vladimir became a convert; but his method of showing it was rather peculiar.

He might have been baptized by the bishop of Kief; or, if he had applied at Constantinople, the emperor would gladly have sent him a high prelate to perform the service. Instead of this, Vladimir collected an army and marched against Kherson,—the last city in Russia held by the Byzantine. It was taken by means of treachery, and from this city Vladimir sent to Constantinople to demand in marriage the sister of the two emperors Basil and Constantine. Although the emperors did not like the proposed connection, they consented because they feared an invasion, but made it a condition that Vladimir should be baptized. The ceremony was performed at Kherson; soon after the bride arrived and the marriage took place in the same city. When he returned to Kief, he carried with him the priests and sacred ornaments taken from the churches of Kherson.

Upon his return to Kief, he began missionary work by his own peculiar methods. His first orders were to pull down the idols; during the execution the people wept, moaned, and wrung their hands. Perun's image was handsomely flogged and thrown into the Dnieper. Since it was made of wood, it soon came to the surface, which was looked upon as a miracle by the people who rushed down to worship it. But Vladimir's soldiers gave it another bath, and this time it was caught by the current and drifted away. The cliff where it stood is still known at Kief as "the devil's leap," and the spot where Perun floated ashore, is shown to visitors.

R. Van Bergen

After thus getting rid of the idols, Vladimir commanded the people of Kief, men, women, and children, to plunge into the Dnieper, which had been consecrated for the occasion, that they might be baptized. When they had obeyed his order, the priests read the service, so that after entering into the river as heathen, they left it as Christians. The people of Novgorod were converted in the same swift and practical manner, since no attention was paid to their objections.

Heathen temples were next converted into churches, which were decorated by Greek artists. Vladimir erected at Kief the church of St. Basil, on the place where Perun's image had stood. Numerous other churches were built; he also founded schools where the Bible was taught in the Slav language. At first the people objected to send their children, because they looked upon reading and writing as magic. But Vladimir had persuasive ways, and was not likely to be deterred by such opposition. Nestor admired him very much. He says that Vladimir was a different man after he had been converted; that he was so afraid of committing a sin, that he hesitated to inflict capital punishment, until the bishop reminded him that crime must be punished. He also divided his income among the churches, and thus became the Saint Vladimir of Russia. Popular ballads keep alive the memory of the first Christian prince. He is often mentioned in them as "The Beautiful Sun" of Kief.

It cannot be supposed that the Russian people were converted at once into good Christians by Vladimir's forceful method. Several centuries were to pass away before the peasants could be induced to part with their heathen customs. The priests preferred to let them remain under a Christian name. There is something mystic in the Slav character. He nurses the belief in magicians and sorcerers, which has never been uprooted. It is seen at present in the worship of the *eikon* or saint's image.

Vladimir died in 1015. He, too, divided Russia among his numerous sons. One of them, Iaroslaf, received Novgorod, where he began to interfere with the rights of the people. A deputation of leading citizens came to him with a protest. He ordered their arrest and condemned them to death. Meanwhile Vladimir's other heirs had indulged in the usual quarrels and wars, until it seemed as if Sviatopolk, a nephew, would become the sole ruler. Iaroslaf then called the principal people of Novgorod together, and threw himself upon their generosity. They forgave him and promised their support. They kept their word, and after a long and bloody war he entered Kief as his father's successor.

Iaroslaf was unfortunate in a war with the Byzantine Empire. The Russian fleet was badly defeated in the Bosphorus; 8,000 men were killed, and 800 prisoners were taken to Constantinople.

Of greater importance was Iaroslaf's work at home. He built churches and monasteries; St. Sophia church was the pride of Kief; the monastery of The Catacombs still draws pilgrims from all parts of Russia. Kief became known as "the city of four hundred churches." He also founded a school for three hundred boys at Novgorod, thereby showing that Russia at that time was second to no European nation.

Kief, under his reign, was one of the most prosperous cities. This was due to her situation on the Dnieper and her trade with the Byzantine Empire, to the great fertility of the Black Earth land, and to Iaroslaf's connection by marriage with the reigning families of Europe. Of his daughters Elizabeth was the wife of the King of Norway, Anne of the King of France, and Anastasia of the King of Hungary; his sister Mary was married to the King of Poland, and his sons had married into royal families. Merchants from Holland, Germany, Hungary, and Scandinavia were established at Kief. The Dnieper was

R. Van Bergen

alive with merchant vessels, and she counted eight markets. It is evident that Iaroslaf took pains to protect and advance commerce. He had coins minted with his Slav name on one side, and his Christian name Ioury (George), on the other.

Perhaps his greatest work is the code of laws established by him, known as the *Russkaia Pravda* or Russian Right. Though necessarily primitive, it was a long step in advance of that time. It followed chiefly the ideas of right and wrong according to the conceptions of the Scandinavians.

At this time, although the dignity of *kniaz*, duke or prince, was hereditary in the family of Rurik, it was understood by all parties that the reign of the prince depended upon the consent of his subjects, and perhaps more still upon that of his drujina. A story is told that in Vladimir's time the drujina complained that they were made to eat from wooden bowls, whereupon he gave them silver ones, saying: I could not buy myself a drujina with gold and silver; but with a drujina, I can acquire gold and silver, as did my father and my grandfather.

Ever since Kief had been the residence of Rurik's descendants, they had been recognized as Grand Dukes, because they represented the eldest of the descendants. They did not, as a rule, interfere with the administration, but were the dukes, the commanders of the armies. Many districts had such a duke, who was, however, invariably of the blood of Rurik, and recognized the superior authority as the eldest of the blood. When the Grand Duke of Kief died, he was not succeeded by his son, unless he had neither uncle nor brother living; but it was within the power of the grand duke to leave one or more districts to his sons.

The descendants of the Norsemen were, therefore, the defenders of the districts which they ruled as dukes.

Novgorod and Pskof were republics on the northwest frontier, and usually had the same duke. Smolensk was an important dukedom, because it contained the sources of the Volga, the Dnieper, and the Dwina, and embraced the ancient forest of Okof. Not far from it was the dukedom of Toropetz. On the Upper Oka was Tchernigof—a rival of Kief; further to the south was Novgorod-Swerki, and east of the Upper Don, extending as far as the Oka, were Riazan and Mourom. The dukedom of Souzdal, inhabited by a mixture of Finns and Slavs, was in the north, the soil still covered by forests. Southeast Russia embraced Red Russia, that is Volhynia and Gallicia Proper.

The introduction of the Greek Church caused important changes. The Greek Priests could not comprehend the relation between the people and its defenders. To them the duke was not a *dux* (leader), but a Caesar, Kaiser, or Czar, ruling, not with the consent of the governed, but by the grace of God, as did the emperors at Constantinople. This idea gradually penetrated into the minds of the several dukes, until it was accepted and enforced by them.

Another very important change was effected by the Greek religion. We have seen that according to the old Slav customs, it was not the son who succeeded as the head of the family, but its eldest member. It appears that the same custom prevailed among the Norsemen, as we have seen that it was Rurik's brother, and not his son who succeeded him. In the Byzantine Empire, the oldest son was the heir, and the priests tried to introduce this as a law.

As the descendants of Rurik increased in number, it was not always easy to determine who was entitled to the succession. Hence there were often several claimants, and as a result, civil wars followed. These wars, strange as it may appear, served to bind the dukedoms together, because most of them were waged for the purpose of establishing the claim of a duke upon the possession of Kief.

Iaroslaf died in 1054, and was buried in the church of St. Sophia at Kief. In his will we see the effect of the Greek Church, for he specially appointed his eldest son Isiaslaf as his successor. A younger brother, Sviatoslaf, took up arms, and expelled him in 1073. Upon his death in 1076, Isiaslaf returned to Kief, where he lived two years. He died in 1078, and was succeeded by his brother Vsevolod, who was grand duke until 1093, when he was succeeded by Sviatopolk, the son of Isiaslaf, as the eldest of the family. He was not opposed by Vsevolod's famous son Vladimir Monomachus, who admitted that Sviatopolk's "father was older than mine, and reigned first in Kief."

V

A RUSSIAN REPUBLIC

Sviatopolk reigned from 1093 to 1113. It was at this time that Russia was disturbed by two civil wars. At the instance of Vladimir Monomachus a congress of dukes met in 1097, at Loubetch on the Dnieper to discuss the folly of civil wars which placed the country at the mercy of its enemies. An agreement was concluded, wherein the dukes swore upon the Cross that "henceforth the Russian land shall be considered the country of us all, and whoso shall dare arm himself against his brother, shall be our common enemy."

Soon after this a quarrel broke out about the succession of Volhynia, and again the country was plunged into civil strife, which lasted two years. In 1100 another congress was held at Vititchevo, on the left bank of the Dnieper, where the dispute was settled, and it was resolved to unite in a war with a powerful nomad people. The Russians under Vladimir Monomachus gained a brilliant victory; the nomads had seventeen khans killed on the battlefield.

When Sviatopolk died, the people of Kief declared that they would have no grand duke except Vladimir. He declined saying that there were elder heirs entitled to the succession; but when troubles broke out in the city, he gave his consent.

R. Van Bergen

During his reign of twelve years, from 1113 to 1125, Kief reached the height of prosperity and power. He reduced Souzdal, in the north, to submission, and made many improvements. His memory is cherished in Russia. He compiled a set of instructions for his sons, from which we may judge of his character. Among other remarks, he says: "It is neither by fasting, nor solitude, nor the life in a cloister that will procure for you the life eternal,—it is doing good. Do not forget the poor but feed them. Do not bury your wealth in the bosom of the earth, for that is contrary to the precepts of Christianity. Be a father to orphans, judge the cause of widows yourself." "Put to death no one be he innocent or guilty, for nothing is more precious than the soul of a Christian." "When you have learned anything useful, try to preserve it in your memory, and strive ceaselessly to acquire knowledge. Without ever leaving his palace, my father spoke five languages, *a thing that foreigners admire in us.*"

There are in the museum at Moscow, a throne and crown, supposed to have belonged to this noble and patriotic duke; unfortunately it has been shown that they were never in his possession.

In his will, Vladimir gave the dukedom of Souzdal to his son George Dolgorouki, and another son, Mstislaf, succeeded as grand duke at Kief. When the latter died in 1146, leaving the grand dukedom to his son Isiaslaf, George Dolgorouki claimed the succession as the eldest of the family. Both sides were supported by their friends, and some fierce battles were fought, but Isiaslaf maintained himself until his death in 1157. After his reign, Kief's importance began to decrease. Twelve years later, in 1169, it was captured by the Russians of the north. A native historian[1] says of this event: "This mother of Russian cities had been many times besieged and oppressed. She had often opened her Golden Gate to her enemies, but none had ever yet entered by force. To their eternal shame, the victors forgot that they, too, were Russians! During three days not only the houses, but the cloisters, churches, and even the temples of St. Sophia and the Dime, were given over to pillage. The precious images, the sacerdotal ornaments, the books, and the bells,—all were carried off."

[Footnote 1: Karamsin.]

With the fall of Kief, the scene of Russian activity shifts to the north. There, in the dukedom of Souzdal, George Dolgorouki laid, in 1147, the foundation of a town, Moscow, on a height overlooking the Moscowa. For many years it remained an obscure village, and gave no sign of its future greatness.

The chief interest at this time centers about the Russian republics, Novgorod, Pskof, and Viatka. Although Novgorod did not possess the advantages of Kief, since its soil was sandy, marshy, and unproductive, the enterprise of its people made it the wealthiest and most populous city of Russia. It is recorded that it counted 100,000 inhabitants, when Rurik arrived in Russia. He and his immediate successors were satisfied with the position of Defender, which suited their warlike and blunt character, and with the revenues assigned to them, which with the spoils taken from the enemy, were ample for their wants. These republics were administered by a vetche or municipal council, with a possadnik or burgo-master, whose duty it was to see that the city's privileges were preserved, and who distributed the taxes. He shared with the duke in the administration of justice. There was a militia for the defense of the people's rights, commanded by a *tysatski*. Every ward of the city had a *starost*, charged with preserving the peace. It is said that a written constitution, partaking of the nature of the Magna Charta, was granted to

Novgorod by Iaroslaf the Great. The duke's rights and privileges, his duties and his revenues, were carefully set down. He was entitled to the tribute of some of the volosts,—cantons or counties,—and to certain fines; he could gather in his harvests at stated times, and was not permitted to hunt in the forest except in the autumn. He could neither execute nor annul a judgment without the approval of the possadnik, and he was expressly forbidden to carry a lawsuit beyond Novgorod. Every duke, before he entered upon his office, was compelled to take an oath to this constitution.

The members of the vetche were elected by a unanimous vote, instead of by a majority. This gave rise to frequent, and sometimes very serious disorder, because if a minority did not approve of the candidate, they were apt to be ill-treated. There were occasions when two rival vetches were elected, and when this happened in the two parts of the city divided by the river Volkhof, the bridge between them was often the scene of a free fight. Owing to the extensive trade connections, the merchants trading with western Europe by way of the Baltic sought to promote friendly relations with the dukes of the west, who had it in their power to promote or obstruct their trade; but the merchants dealing with Asia, and those who connected with Constantinople had other interests to consider and to guard. Thus there were often three parties, each concerned with its own interests, and forgetting that their prosperity was first and chiefly dependent upon the power of the republic, they rendered it an easy prey for an ambitious duke. The people, however, boasted of their patriotism, and during the early period they were strong enough to defy the duke. On some occasions, he and his drujina were expelled, or, as they expressed it, "the people made him a reverence, and showed him a way to leave." Sometimes, too, it happened that the duke was made a prisoner, and confined in the Archbishop's palace. When

Sviatopolk was Grand Duke of Kief (1093-1113), he wished to force one of his sons upon the people of Novgorod. "Send him along," said they, "if he has a head to spare!" Usually the duke was glad to leave Novgorod, if he could secure another dukedom. In 1132, Vsevolod Gabriel left Novgorod to become Duke of Pereiaslaf, hoping to succeed as Grand Duke of Kief. Seeing no way to attain the coveted dignity, he signified his wish to return to the people of Novgorod. "You have forgotten your oath to die with us," they replied; "you have sought another dukedom; now you may go where you please." In this case, however, the people changed their mind, and did take him back; but four years afterwards they expelled him, declaring that "he took no care of the poor people; he desired to establish himself at Pereiaslaf; at the battle of Mount Idanof against the men of Souzdal, he and his drujina were the first to leave the battlefield; he was fickle in the quarrels of the dukes, sometimes joining one party and sometimes the other."

So long as the descendants of Rurik remained satisfied with their position, Novgorod had enough men and resources to maintain its independence; but more than that was required after the dukes had tasted of the sweets of unlimited power.

George Dolgorouki had established colonies in Souzdal. The land was his, the colonists were his subjects. He was no longer merely the defender, he was the owner, not the duke, but the prince. There was no vetche or popular assembly in his possessions. His son, Andrew Bogolioubski, was brought up and educated amid these conditions, more in conformity with those prevailing in Greece and other parts of Europe, where the people were supposed to exist for the sole benefit of their prince. It was he who ruined Kief, and the fall of that city foretold the doom of Novgorod. "The fall of Kief," says a Russian author,[2] "seemed to foreshadow the loss of Novgorod liberty; it was the same army, and it was the same

R. Van Bergen

prince who commanded it. But the people of Kief, accustomed to change their masters,—to sacrifice the vanquished to the victors,—only fought for the honor of their dukes, while those of Novgorod were to shed their blood for the defense of the laws and institutions established by their ancestors."

[Footnote 2: Karamsin.]

During his father's life, Andrew left his castle on the Dnieper, and moved northward to Vladimir which town he enlarged, and where he founded a quarter named Bogolioubovo, whence his name of Bogolioubski. After the death of George Dolgorouki, Andrew first made a successful campaign against the Bulgarians, and then, after sacking Kief, he turned his attention toward Novgorod, where he had established one of his nephews. The cause of the quarrel is not known, but Andrew began by compelling the neighboring dukes to join him, and overran the territory of the republic with fire and sword. The people of Novgorod, remembering the fate of Kief, were prepared to die in the defense of the city. The siege commenced. One day the Archbishop took the eikon—image—of the Virgin, which was carried around in solemn procession. It was struck by an arrow shot by a Souzdalian soldier, when miraculous tears appeared upon its face. The besiegers were struck by a panic, and the people of Novgorod sallied out, killed a number of the enemy, and took so many prisoners that "you could get six Souzdalians for a grivna." Whatever may have been the value of that coin, the market was evidently overstocked with Souzdalians.

Foiled in this attempt, Andrew tried other means. He prohibited the sale of grain to the people of Novgorod, who were thereby compelled to make peace. They did not surrender any of their privileges but accepted as their duke the prince selected by Andrew.

His next war was with Mstislaf the Brave, Duke of Smolensk, who, aided by his brothers, had taken Kief. Andrew sent a herald to him demanding the evacuation of Kief, and imposing a fine upon each brother. Mstislaf who, the Russians say, "feared none but God," gave orders to have the herald's head and beard shaved,—a gross insult at that time,—and then dismissed him, saying: "Go and repeat these words unto your master,—'Up to this time we have respected you like a father, but since you do not blush to treat us as your vassals and common people, since you have forgotten that you speak to princes, we laugh at your threats. Execute them!—we appeal to the judgment of God.'" The challenge was accepted, and Andrew was defeated.

The Duke of Souzdal did not relax in his attempts to established absolute government. It was with this purpose in view that he expelled his three brothers, and made friends of the priests. Kief was still the residence of the *Metropolitan* or head of the Greek Church in Russia, and Andrew was anxious that he should transfer his residence to Vladimir so as to make that city the religious center of Russia. His wish was not gratified. He failed in everything, except in making enemies by his disregard of law. He was murdered in 1174 in his favorite palace at Bogolioubovo, by his own *boyards* or nobles.

VI

TROUBLOUS TIMES

The death of Andrew was a welcome relief for the people of Novgorod. They celebrated it by attacking the houses of the rich, and committed so many excesses that the priests made a procession with the eikons. In Souzdal there was trouble about the succession. Two of Andrew's brothers returned from exile, and claimed the dukedom, and the city of Vladimir gave them its support. That was enough for Souzdal and Rostof to recognize another claimant, one of Andrew's nephews. Vladimir was victorious in the contest, and Andrew's brother, Michael, became Grand Duke of Souzdal. He died two years afterwards, and the people of Souzdal once more refused to recognize Vladimir's candidate, Andrew's other brother Vsevolod, surnamed the Big Nest on account of his numerous family. Vladimir defeated Souzdal and Vsevolod was its grand duke from 1176 to 1212. The people of Novgorod thought best to pacify him. They sent a deputation to Vladimir, to tell Vsevolod, "Lord and Grand Duke, our country is your patrimony; we entreat you to send us the grandson of George Dolgorouki, the great-grandson of Monomachus, to govern us." The request was granted, and Vsevolod's eldest son Constantine came to Novgorod. The grand duke, however, was soon displeased with him and displaced him by a younger son,

Iaroslaf. Soon there were quarrels between him and the people, whereupon Iaroslaf moved to Torjok, a town within Novgorod territory, and from there stopped all supplies. Famine appeared in the city, and at last envoys were sent to the duke, who had them arrested. Nothing except absolute submission would satisfy him. In this dire need help came from an unexpected quarter. Mstislaf the Bold, son of Mstislaf the Brave, Duke of Smolensk, heard of Novgorod's plight and sent word to the city, "Torjok shall not hold itself higher than Novgorod. I will deliver your lands and citizens, or leave my bones among you." He was as good as his word. There was a great war between Souzdal and Smolensk; no quarter was asked or given. In 1216, Vsevolod's sons were attacked at Lipetsk by the troops of Novgorod and Smolensk, with such fury that they were routed, and 9,000 were killed whereas only 60 were taken prisoners. Iaroslaf renounced Novgorod and released the citizens arrested by him.

Constantine succeeded his father Vsevolod, but died in 1217, and another brother, George, became Grand Duke of Souzdal. This prince made an expedition down the Volga, levying tribute as he proceeded. In 1220, he laid the foundation of Nishni Novgorod, and of several villages in what was then Moravian territory.

Meanwhile Mstislaf the Bold resigned as Grand Duke of Novgorod in an assembly of the people, saying, "I salute St. Sophia, the tomb of my father,[3] and you. People of Novgorod, I am going to reconquer Galitch from the strangers, but I shall never forget you. I hope I may lie by the tomb of my father in St. Sophia." The people implored him to remain; but he had made up his mind, and in 1218 he left for the southwest, where he did succeed in conquering Galitch, that is the name given to southwestern Russia at that time.

R. Van Bergen

[Footnote 3: Mstislaf the Brave was buried in the church of St. Sophia.]

After his departure the people of Novgorod called his nephew Sviatoslaf as their grand duke, but soon there was a quarrel. The possadnik Tferdislaf caused the arrest of one of the wealthy citizens, whose friends rose to set him free. Then the burgomaster's friends came and there was a fight in which ten men were killed. The grand duke then demanded the dismissal of the burgomaster, and the vetche assembled to hear both sides. The grand duke was asked what crime the possadnik had committed.

"None," he replied, "but it is my will that he be dismissed."

The burgomaster then said: "I am satisfied, because I am not accused of any fault; as for you, my brothers, you can dismiss alike possadniks and dukes."

The vetche consulted, and announced its decision:

"Prince, since you do not accuse the possadnik of any fault, remember that you have sworn to depose no magistrate without trial. Tferdislaf will remain our possadnik,—we will not deliver him to you."

Sviatoslaf was very much displeased and resigned, and one of his brothers, Vsevolod, was appointed in his place. This was in 1219; two years later, in 1221, Vsevolod was expelled, and the people called back that same Iaroslaf from whom they had been rescued by Mstislaf the Bold. Soon there was another dispute and *he* was sent about his business. Vsevolod of Smolensk was again made duke, but the people soon grew tired of him. At this time the Grand Duke of Souzdal interfered; he made Novgorod pay him tribute, and appointed a prince of Tchernigof as its duke; but he did not like the place and resigned. Then the city suffered from a famine, when 42,000 citizens perished and a fire destroyed a whole quarter of the city. Iaroslaf was made duke for the fourth time; the spirit of the people was broken, and he was permitted to rule over them as he pleased. He succeeded as grand duke in 1236, when he left his son Alexander Nevski as duke in Novgorod.

The east coast of the Baltic was considered tributary to Novgorod. Several colonies had been established on the Duena and south of that river, but in the 12th and 13th centuries missionaries and merchants from Germany appeared and gradually penetrated as far as the Duena where Bishop Meinhard, in 1187, built a Roman Catholic Church and a fortress. The Livonians were converted much as St. Vladimir had made Christians of the people of Kief; but in this case, the people of Livonia revolted; in 1198 the second bishop was killed in battle, and the natives returned to the heathen gods. Pope Innocent III ordered a crusade against them. Another bishop sailed up the Duena with a fleet of twenty-three ships, and in 1200 founded Riga. The year after a religious society, the Sword-bearers, resembling the Templars, was installed in Livonia, and the natives appealed to the Duke of Polotsk for help. They marched upon Riga and were defeated in 1206.

German colonization proceeded actively under the Sword-bearers. Several cities were founded, and the country was divided into fiefs, according to the feudal system of Western Europe. The towns were modeled after Hamburg, Bremen, and Luebeck. Riga grew into a large and powerful city.

In 1225, another religious-brotherhood, the Teutonic Order, entered into Lithuania, and twelve years later the two orders united. The introduction of the Roman Catholic religion carried with it the elements of Roman civilization, and did

R. Van Bergen

much toward estranging the natives of the Baltic provinces from the Russians of the east.

Southwestern Russia, or Galitch, had, more than any other section, preserved the old Slav character. "The duke was a prince of the old Slavonic type. He was elected by a popular assembly, and kept his seat by its consent."[4] The assembly was composed of boyards or nobles, and sometimes disputes occurred between them and the duke, which ended in more or less serious disorders. In 1188, the position was offered to Roman, Duke of Volhynia. He accepted, but before he could enter the capital, a duke who had been expelled was reinstalled. After his death, Roman entered the territory of Galitch, not as an elected duke, but as a conqueror at the head of an army, and treated the dukedom as a conquest. He was especially cruel to the boyards, treating their rights and privileges with scorn. Russian authors praise him; one of them says that he "walked in the ways of God, exterminated the heathen, flung himself like a lion upon the infidels, *was savage as a wild cat, deadly as a crocodile*, swooped down on his prey like an eagle," which seem strange qualities for praise. Roman died in battle, in 1205. Mstislaf the Bold conquered Galitch and at his death, in 1228, his son-in-law Daniel became duke.

[Footnote 4: Kostomarof.]

We have seen that, in the 13th century, Russia was divided into a number of small states, most of them under a duke, but all possessing some degree of liberty, except in the north where the duke was being changed into an hereditary monarch. We have also seen that Russia was part of Europe, and that commercial relations were maintained. At the same time, just as there had been an invisible but none the less real dividing line between the Eastern Roman, or Byzantine, Empire and the west of Europe, so with the adoption of the

Greek Church, Russia inherited the oriental type and principles which separated that form of Christianity from that of Rome. Thus the slight split grew gradually into a schism, as Western Europe progressed with every evolution of the Roman Church, whereas Russia remained stationary.

Byzantium or Constantinople, situated at the easternmost edge of Europe, owing to its intimate association with the Persians who, at the time represented the Oriental character, was more of an oriental than a western city; its sympathies were also with its neighbors of the east. There was thus an oriental tendency in Russia as well as in the Byzantine Empire, and this vague sentiment enabled Russia to bend before a blast, which would have withered any nation of a more pronounced occidental character.

R. Van Bergen

VII

THE YELLOW PERIL

On the borders of the Chinese Empire, in the northeast of Asia, roamed a Mongol tribe, known as the Tartars or Tatars. A Chinese author of that time, described them as follows: "The Ta-tzis[5] or Das occupy themselves exclusively with their flocks; they go wandering ceaselessly from pasture to pasture, from river to river. They are ignorant of the nature of a town or a wall. They are ignorant of writing and books; their treaties are concluded orally. From infancy they are accustomed to ride, to aim their arrows at rats and birds, and thus acquire the courage essential to their life of wars and destruction. They have neither religious ceremonies nor judicial institutions. From the prince to the lowest among the people, all are fed by the flesh of the animals whose skin they use for clothing. The strongest among them have the largest and fattest morsels at feasts; the old men are put off with the fragments that are left. They respect nothing but strength and courage; age and weakness are condemned."

[Footnote 5: Ta, great; hence: the Great Tzis.]

The people were, therefore, nomads, moving their flocks as necessity required, and occasionally making a raid upon a neighboring town. "They move on horseback;" says the

Chinese author; "when they wish to capture a town, they fall on the suburban villages. Each leader seizes ten men, and every prisoner is forced to carry a certain quantity of wood, stones, and other material. They use these for filling up moats or to dig trenches. In the capture of a town the loss of a myriad men was thought nothing. No place could resist them. After a siege, the entire population was massacred, without distinction of old or young, rich or poor, beautiful or ugly, those who resisted or those who yielded; no distinguished person escaped death, if a defense was attempted."

These nomad Tartars were united by and under Genghis Khan (1154-1227), one of their chiefs or khans. He summoned all the khans of the several tribes, and before them took the title of emperor over all, declaring that, as there was only one sun in heaven, so there should be but one emperor on earth. At the head of his tribes, Genghis conquered Manchuria and North China; then he moved west. He himself remained in Asia, but two of his lieutenants proceeded in that direction, subduing the tribes on their way, and often joined by them. The long march had rendered the Tartars inured to hardship and wholly indifferent to danger. At last they passed by the southern shore of the Caspian Sea, and, crossing the Caucasus, commenced the invasion of Europe.

The march of such a host could not be kept secret. When the Polovtsi, the old enemies of Russia, heard of the approach, they sent for help to the Christian dukes. "When they have taken our country, they will take yours," they said. Mstislaf the Bold of Galitch, urged that the assistance be granted, and the chief of the Polovtsi agreed to enter the Greek Church. The Russians assembled on the lower Dnieper, where they were approached by some Tatar envoys who told them that they had "come by God's command against our slaves and grooms, the accursed Polovtsi. Be at peace with us; we have no quarrel with you." The envoys were arrested and put to death. The Russian army then moved eastward, and met the Tartar host at the Kalka, a small river running into the Sea of Azof. Instead of waiting for the troops still on the way, Mstislaf the Bold and his friends began the battle. While it was at its height, the Polovtsi were seized by a panic and, falling back, threw the Russians into disorder. The Russian army was routed; six dukes and seventy high boyards were left dead on the battlefield, and hardly a tenth of the army escaped. The Grand Duke of Kief still occupied a fortified camp on the Kalka. The Tartars offered to allow him and his drujina to retire upon payment of a ransom. He accepted, and was attacked by the Tartars after he had left his fortifications. He and his two sons were stifled under boards, and his guard was massacred.

The Tartars at this time needed all their men to complete the conquest of China, and therefore the armies invading Europe were recalled, after southern Russia was at their mercy. The Russians did not inquire into the cause of this relief, but resumed their old life, confident that all danger was past.

When the Tartars had made themselves masters of China, Bati, a nephew of Genghis, was dispatched westward to mark further conquests. He did not follow the same route but passed south of the Ural Mountains. Thirteen years after the battle of the Kalka, Bati besieged and took the capital of the Bulgars, east of the grand dukedom of Souzdal (1237). As soon as the dukes of Central Russia heard this, they united against the Tartars, but the Grand Duke of Souzdal refused to join them. The Tartars sent envoys to the allied dukes. "If you want peace," they said, "give us the tenth of your goods." "When we are dead," was the proud reply, "you can have the whole." A battle was fought in which the Russians were crushed. Nearly all the dukes died on the battlefield; Riazan was stormed, sacked, and burned, and the other towns of that dukedom met the same fate.

It was now the turn of Souzdal. The army of the grand duke was defeated on the Oka; Moscow was burned and Vladimir besieged. After an heroic defense, the Tartars took the city by assault, and many Russians were burned in the cathedral which was set on fire. Leaving ruin in their wake, the Tartars went in search of the grand duke who had taken a position on the Sit, near the frontiers of Novgorod. Here another battle was fought ending in disaster for the Russians. The headless corpse of the grand duke was found by the Bishop of Rostof. On swept the Asiatic hoards, as if nothing would stop them. At Torjok, "Russian heads fell beneath the sword of the Tartars as grass beneath the scythe." Leaving Souzdal behind, they entered the territory of Novgorod; but the dense forests and swollen rivers delayed them, and when within fifty miles of the city, they turned southeast. The little town of Kozelsk[6] did not surrender but inflicted such a loss upon the invaders that they mentioned it as "the wicked city." When it was captured, every man, woman, and child, was butchered.

[Footnote 6: Where Kalouga now stands.]

The years 1239 and 1240 were spent in ravaging southern Russia. Pereiaslaf and Tchernigof, after a desperate defense, were burned, and the Tartars under command of Genghis's grandson Mangou, marched upon Kief. Mangou offered terms, but Kief, knowing the fate of other cities, executed Mangou's envoys. The grand duke and his rival, Daniel of Galitch, fled from the city, but the people fought for their lives. Mangou was reenforced by Bati's army and the siege began. The walls were knocked to pieces by battering rams. "The people of Kief, led by the brave Dmitri, a Gallician boyard, defended the battered ramparts till the end of the day, and then retreated to the Church of the Dime, which they surrounded by a palisade. The last defenders of Kief were grouped round the tomb of Iaroslaf. The next day they perished. Mangou gave the boyard his life, but the Mother of Russian Cities was sacked. This third pillage was the most terrible; even the tombs were not respected. All that remains of the Church of the Dime is only a few fragments of mosaic in the museum at Kief. Saint Sophia and the Monastery of the Catacombs were delivered up to be plundered." Kief fell in 1240.

There remained only Volhynia and Gallicia, which also bowed under the Tartar yoke. With the exception of Novgorod and the northwest, Russia was in possession of the Yellow race. The Russian dukes who had escaped carried the tale to Western Europe which was soon in a state of alarm. The Emperor of Germany wrote to the other monarchs: "This is the moment to open the eyes of body and soul, now that the brave princes on whom we depended are dead or in slavery." The Pope called upon the Christian princes to take up arms. Meanwhile Bati continued his westward march and penetrated as far as Moravia, when he was recalled by the death of the second Tartar emperor. He withdrew to Russia and on the Volga built a city which he named Sarai—the Castle,—which became the capital of a Tartar empire extending from the Ural river and Caspian Sea to the mouth of the Danube, and is known as the Golden Horde.

The first three successors of Genghis Khan are known as the Great Khans, and ruled over all the Tartars; but after Kublai Khan established himself in China, in 1260, the Golden Horde declared its independence. So long as Bati lived, this khanate was united and powerful, but after his death, in 1257, it gradually lost strength. In 1272, these Tartars became Mahomedans and spread that faith. The Golden Horde enjoyed another period of prosperity under the Khan Uzbeck.

How did the Russians bear this blow? We have seen that Iaroslaf, the duke who had been expelled so many times from Novgorod, became Grand Duke of Souzdal. He found the country in Souzdal in ruins. Nothing was left of the towns and villages but charred remains; the inhabitants who had survived the Tartar massacres had fled into the forests. Iaroslaf's first work was to induce them to return and rebuild their homes. The Tartar general Bati heard of this and sent word to Iaroslaf to come to him. The grand duke dared not refuse. He went to Sarai on the Volga where Bati told him that he might continue as grand duke, but that it would be best for him to pay a visit to the great khan, who was then on the Amoor in the far eastern part of Asia. Iaroslaf agreed; he started on his long journey, and after many months of travel through deserts and wastes, he arrived at the headquarters of the Tartars. There he was compelled to kneel before Oktai, the successor of Genghis. It appears that some Russian boyards had preceded Iaroslaf hoping to secure favors from the khan, and that they accused the grand duke, but Oktai refused to listen to them. After some delay Iaroslaf was confirmed as grand duke, and permitted to return, but he died from exhaustion in the desert, in 1246. His remains were brought to Vladimir.

Iaroslaf left two sons, Andrew, who succeeded him in Souzdal, and Alexander who was duke at Novgorod. This younger son was an able as well as a brave man. On one occasion, when the Scandinavians had invaded Novgorod's territory aided by the Catholic Orders, Alexander had gained a great victory on the Neva, from which he is known in history as Alexander Nevski (1240). Upon his return to Novgorod he had a dispute with the vetche, and he left the city. After his departure the territory of the Republic was invaded by the German Sword-bearers who erected a fort on the Neva, captured Pskof, Novgorod's ally, and plundered merchants within a short distance of the walls. The people

R. Van Bergen

sent to Alexander Nevski, begging him to come to their rescue, and after several refusals he consented. Alexander collected an army, drove the Germans out of Pskof and their new fort, and at last defeated them on the ice of Lake Peipus in 1242. This is known as the Battle on the Ice. Alexander then returned to Novgorod where he was received with honor and joy.

Andrew, the Grand Duke of Souzdal, Alexander's brother, refused to recognize Bati's authority, whereupon a Tartar army ravaged his territory for the second time. Novgorod, as we have seen, had escaped the Tartar invasion, but when Alexander Nevski received a letter from Bati, in which the khan said, "God has subjected many peoples to me, will you alone refuse to recognize my power? If you wish to keep your land, come to me; you will see the splendor and the glory of my government." The duke thought it prudent to comply. He and his brother Andrew went to Sarai, where honors were showered upon the hero of the Neva. The two brothers were directed to visit the great khan, as their father Iaroslaf had done. They did so; and the Mongol emperor confirmed Andrew as Duke of Souzdal, but to Alexander's dukedom, he added Kief and South Russia. They returned from the Far East in 1257.

VIII

RUSSIA UNDER THE MONGOL YOKE

The Tartars did not interfere with the people, their institutions, or religion, but they demanded tribute in the form of
an annual poll-tax. Officers called baskaks went from house
to house to collect it, either in money or in furs, and those
who could not pay were sold as slaves. Sometimes this
collection caused disturbances. It was some time before the
people of Novgorod would submit. When Bati sent his
collectors to the Republic, the question was brought before
the vetche where the possadnik urged the wisdom of paying
the tax, but the people would not hear of it and promptly
murdered the unfortunate burgomaster. Alexander, too,
advised to avoid trouble, but the people refused and several
boyards, including Alexander's son Vassili urged resistance.
The duke acted vigorously. He ordered the arrest of his son,
and had the boyards punished; but it was not before the
people heard of the approach of a Tartar army, that they
submitted. Still such was their resentment that Alexander had
the baskaks guarded night and day. At last Alexander
threatened to leave Novgorod with his drujina; then the
people offered no further opposition to the collection of the
hated poll-tax (1260). Two years later the people of Souzdal,
Vladimir, and Rostof rose against the baskaks and killed one
of them, a Russian who had become a Mahomedan.

R. Van Bergen

Alexander, who had succeeded his brother Andrew as Grand Duke, decided to attempt to appease the khan by going himself to Sarai with presents; he also wished to be excused from furnishing a body of Russians to serve in the Tartar army. He succeeded, but was kept at the court of the khan for a year. His health broke down and he died on his return journey in 1263. The news of his death was brought to Novgorod, as mass was being said in the cathedral. The Metropolitan who was reading the service, interrupted it, and said, "Learn, my dear children, that the Sun of Russia has set,—is dead," and the people cried, "We are lost." The death of Alexander Nevski was a heavy blow to Russia.

The Russians, that is the people of Russia whose story we are reading, did not mingle with any Tartar except the tax collector whom they did not like. The victors were nomads, who did not care to occupy the land they had conquered. When they did settle at Sarai on the Lower Volga, they absorbed the tribes who had lived there before the invasion, and who were not Russians, but nomads. The Russian *people* did not associate with the conquerors. It was at this time that the word *Krestianine* or "true Christian" was applied to the peasant, instead of the contemptuous term moujik.

Whatever Asiatic characteristics were grafted upon the Russians, came to them through their kniazes and boyards. The dukes soon showed that all they cared for, was to hold their positions. After Alexander Nevski, there is not a single instance of a desire to relieve the people; and the victors on their part never interfered so long as the tribute was paid regularly. The descendants of Andrew Bogolioubski were not disturbed in Souzdal; those of Roman continued to hold Galitch and Volhynia, and Oleg's house remained in possession of Tchernigof. The dukes might fight about Kief; Novgorod might appoint or expel its dukes,—the Tartars did not mind. But the khan did insist that the dukes should visit him and pay him homage. He also reserved the right of approving the succession of a duke, who was compelled to apply for a written consent, called an *iarlikh*. On one occasion when the people of Novgorod elected Duke Michael, they afterwards refused to recognize him, asserting that "it is true we have chosen Michael, but on condition that he should show us the iarlikh."

The dukes, holding their possessions by favor of the khan, tried to gain his good-will and favor. Gleb, duke of Bielozersk married in the khan's family about 1272; Feodor of Riazan was the son-in-law of the khan of the Nogais. In 1318, the Grand Duke George married Kontchaka, sister of the Khan Uzbeck. It was the rulers, and not the people of Russia, that quietly submitted to the *Tartartchina* or Mongol yoke.

The khans, while they did not care about the people took care that the dukes should show them slavish respect. In 1303, the dukes were convoked, and when they were assembled a letter from the khan was read, in which they were commanded to stop fighting because the great khan desired to see peace established. Whenever such a letter was brought, the dukes were directed to meet the envoys on foot, prostrate themselves, spread fine carpets under their feet, present them with a cup filled with gold pieces, and listen, kneeling, while the letter was read.

Children of the prairie and the desert, the Tartars had neither a religion nor a civilization to impose upon the Russian people. The khans were tolerant because they did not care. Koiyuk had a Christian chapel near his residence. In 1261, the Khan of Sarai gave permission for the erection of a Greek church in his capital, and he allowed a bishop to reside there. Mangou gave equal privileges to Christians, Jews, and Mahomedans.

The dukes and boyards, paying court to the Tartars, gradually adopted their mode of dressing and, as they became Asiatic in appearance, they came under the influence of Asiatic thought. They dressed in a long caftan or flowing robe, wore a sort of turban on the head, swords and daggers in their belts, and when on horseback, sat in very high saddles with short stirrups. Dukes and boyards thus became semi-Asiatic, and drifted away from the people among whom the national principle was kept alive.

Every succeeding visit to the khan served to increase the intimacy of the dukes and their Asiatic masters. It was not many years before the relation with the great khan was severed, but that with the Golden Horde was kept alive. A writer[7] living at that time, who visited Sarai during Bati's life, gives the following description: "It (the court) is crowded and brilliant. His army consists of 600,000 men, 150,000 of whom are Tartars, and 450,000 strangers, Christians as well as infidels. On Good Friday we were conducted to his tent, between two fires, because the Tartars believe that a fire purifies everything, and robs even poison of its danger. *We had to make many prostrations*, and enter the tent without touching the threshold. Bati was on his throne with one of his wives; his brothers, his children, and the Tartar lords were seated on benches; the rest of the assembly were on the ground, the men on the right, the women on the left.... The khan and the lords of the court emptied from time to time cups of gold and silver, while the musicians made the air ring with their melodies. Bati has a bright complexion; he is affable with his men, but inspires general terror." The same writer visited the court of the great khan, and in his description dwells upon the fact that it was not the Tartars who were most terrible, but the Russian dukes and nobles who accused one another and who sought to destroy their own countrymen by bribing the favorites. It was thus that Duke Michael of Tchernigof was murdered in 1246, and Duke Michael of Tver in 1319, by a Russian hireling of the Grand Duke of Moscow who was present when the foul deed was committed. Servile submission to the khans, a haughty demeanor towards their own people, became the characteristics of the dukes. "The dukes of Moscow," says a Russian author,[8] "took the humble title of servants of the khan, and it was by this means that they became powerful monarchs." An English writer[9] comes to the following evident conclusion: "The first czars of Muscovy were the political descendants, not of the Russian dukes, but of the Tartar khans."

[Footnote 7: Planus Corpinius.]

[Footnote 8: Karamsin.]

[Footnote 9: Wallace.]

A gradual change came over the Golden Horde after the Tartars departed from their nomadic life and settled in and about Sarai. They lost their warlike habits, and with them much of their vigor. They began to farm out the poll-tax, that is, they sold the right to collect the tax to merchants of Khiva, whose oppression was so great that the people of Souzdal revolted in 1262, Koursk in 1284, Kolomna in 1318, and Tver in 1327. But the oppression was greater when the dukes of Moscow farmed this tax, not only from their own subjects, but also from neighboring dukedoms. They were absolutely pitiless in collecting from the poor people as much as they could extort, and this was the disgraceful foundation of their wealth and power. The poll-tax, thereafter, was always a favorite source of revenue in Russia.

Besides this tribute, the dukes were compelled to furnish soldiers to their masters. Soon after the conquest, we read of Russian dukes marching with the Tartars at the head of their drujinas, and of supplying them with infantry. In 1276 Boris of Rostof and others, followed Mangou Khan in the war against the tribes of the Caucasus, and helped to sack the town of Dediakof in Daghestan. This was excusable, because the enemy was an alien; but what can be thought of Prince Andrew, the unworthy son of Alexander Nevski, who, in 1281, induced the Tartars to aid him in pillaging Vladimir, Souzdal, Mourom, Moscow, and Pereiaslaf, and led in profaning churches and convents? In 1284, when two descendants of Oleg were dukes of Koursk, one of them put his brother to death for having insulted the khan, and Russian historians blame not the murderer, but the victim, because he had aroused the khan's anger! In 1327, the dukes of Moscow and Souzdal marched against Tver at the command of their Asiatic master. Such was the influence of the Tartar yoke.

The Russian dukes and their nobles lost not only the principle of patriotism, but also that of personal honor. The unfortunate Russians henceforth were to them, not fellow-countrymen but "*tcherne*" "black people." The khans, with true political instinct looking to the perpetuation of this condition, gained the friendship of the Church, as they had that of the dukes. In 1313, the Khan Uzbeck, at the request of the Metropolitan or head of the Church of Moscow, ordered that the Church should retain its privileges, and that it should not be deprived of its property, because, he says, "these possessions are sacred, as they belong to men whose prayers preserve our lives and strengthen our armies." The churches and convents grew enormously rich. They received gifts of land, and the priests, so bribed, allied themselves with the heathen masters, and aided further in oppressing the people.

The descendants of the dukes and drujinas lost the large and generous impulses of the old Norsemen, to make way for the Asiatic deformities of treachery, cruelty, cunning, and disregard of honor. Whatever came in the way of their own interests, was trampled under foot by fair means or foul. The boyards, too, were tainted by the example of the chiefs. The vast extent of the country, the sparsity of the population, the difficulties in the way of communication, and above all the general ignorance, prevented the appearance of a patriot who might have raised a truly national banner, and shaken off the yoke of the servile lackeys of the Tartars.

R. Van Bergen

IX

LITHUANIA AND MOSCOW

We have seen that the Tartar invasion stopped short of Novgorod, and turned southeast, thus leaving northwest Russia free. What are now known as the Baltic Provinces, was at that time covered with dense forests, inhabited by the Finns or Suomi, the Tchouds, Jmouds, and Lithuanians, all of the same race and speaking the same language, but constantly at war with one another. In the 13th century a chief named Mindvog, after killing his brothers and sons, united the tribes, and made himself master of Lithuania. He then invaded Russia whose dukes, suffering under the Tartar yoke, were unable to withstand him. He captured Grodno and Novogredek, when he was confronted by Alexander Nevsky and Daniel of Volhynia in front, and by the Knights of Livonia in his rear. In this extremity Mindvog sent to the Pope promising that he would be converted in return for his good services. Pope Innocent IV replied by sending a papal legate to Grodno, where Mindvog and his wife were baptized, and he was made King of Lithuania (1252). Soon after he had a dispute with the Livonian Knights to whom he was forced to cede the country of the Jmouds. He again became a pagan and, marching against the Knights, defeated them. Upon his return from this expedition, he was murdered by a chief named Dovmont whom he had injured.

Lithuania again fell into anarchy until another enterprising chief named Gedimin restored order in 1315.

Gedimin invaded Russia, defeated a Russo-Tartar army in 1321, and took Tchernigof and Vladimir. He then went south, where the Russian cities readily opened their gates to him, hoping for relief from the Mongol yoke. He took the old capital Kief, and there had his sons baptized in the Greek church and tried to marry them into the families of Russian dukes. He established his capital at Wilna where he attracted many German artists and mechanics by granting them special privileges. He died a pagan, in 1340, dividing his country among his sons and his brother.

One of his sons, Olgerd, succeeded in getting possession of the whole, and then started upon a career of conquest. He first attacked Novgorod, where one of his brothers had taken refuge, and made conquests east and south, until he reached the Black Sea. Although he was a pagan, Simeon the Proud, Grand Duke of Moscow, gave him his daughter; but this did not prevent Olgerd from waging war with Simeon's successors. In 1368, he defeated the Tartars of the Lower Dnieper, and destroyed Cherson in the Crimea.

When he died he followed Gedimin's example by dividing his territories among his sons, but one of them, Jagellon, became sole ruler by putting his brothers to flight and his uncle to death. At this time the Russian language was adopted and with it the Greek Church, although Jagellon was still a pagan. When he married Hedwiga, the heiress to the Kingdom of Poland, he embraced the Roman Catholic church; in 1386, he went to Cracow, where he was crowned King of Poland, and soon after gave orders that his people must join the same church, converting them as Vladimir had introduced Christianity among the people of Kief. Jagellon made Cracow his capital. Some time afterwards one of his

R. Van Bergen

cousins, Vitovt, raised a revolt against him in Lithuania, and Jagellon was compelled to cede that territory to him. Thus Vitovt became Grand Duke of Lithuania.

Vitovt married the sister of Vassili, Grand Duke of Moscow, and extended his domain toward the east. He invaded Smolensk, whose Grand Duke Sviatoslaf, when fighting in Russia, had taken a delight in impaling and burning alive Russian women and children. That savage had been killed in 1387, in a battle with the Lithuanians, and his son had succeeded him. Vitovt, before Smolensk, invited this prince and his brothers to visit him in his tent. They accepted and were warmly received, but when they were ready to depart, they were told that they were prisoners of war. Smolensk was taken by surprise, and pillaged.

Vitovt contemplated the conquest of Russia. His territory bordered in the east on Souzdal and Riazan. He had defeated an army of Tartars in the south, and was making preparations for a bold stroke. Collecting an army of Lithuanians, Poles, Russians, and five hundred Knights of the Teutonic Order, he set out from Kief and came upon the Tartar army near Pultowa where, in 1399, he suffered a serious defeat. He recovered from this blow, and after some time began a war with the Teutonic Order which he defeated in 1410, at the battle of the Tannenberg. He thereupon re-annexed the Jmoud country.

Vitovt had given up his designs upon Russia; he planned to raise Lithuania into a kingdom, and to have a Metropolitan of its own, instead of being dependent upon the head of the Greek Church at Moscow. He succeeded in the last-named object, but met with a check in the former, and, as he was eighty years old, the disappointment caused an illness from which he died, in 1430. After his death, Lithuania had no more influence upon Russia. Sometimes it had a grand duke of its own, at other times it was united with Poland. In 1501, it became the property of the King of Poland, who added to his title that of Grand Duke of Lithuania. Its nobles spoke the Polish language.

It was necessary to sketch in a few words the history of Lithuania, not only because it is part of Russia to-day, but because it has always been claimed by Russia. The history of that country, however, from the beginning of the 14th century, is centered about Muscovia, the territory of the Grand Duke of Moscow. At the time of the Lithuanian conquest, Muscovia was bounded on the north by Tver, on the east by Souzdal, on the south by Riazan, and on the west by Lithuania. It belonged to Alexander Nevski, who at his death left it to his son Daniel. Its area was increased by him by the towns of Pereiaslaf, Zabiesski and Kolomna. Daniel died in 1303, and was buried in the church of St. Michael the Archangel, which remained the burial place of the Muscovite princes until the time of Peter the Great.

The next grand duke was Daniel's son George, whose first act was to capture the Duke of Smolensk from whom he took the town of Mojaisk. In 1304 the Grand Duke of Souzdal died. Michael of Tver claimed the succession as the eldest of the family, but George of Moscow contested it. Michael was supported by the boyards of Vladimir and the people of Novgorod; the khan at Sarai also declared in his favor, and Michael was installed. George, however, was not satisfied and began a war; he was defeated in battle, and twice besieged in Moscow. Suddenly he heard that the khan was dead; he hastened to Sarai, and there made friends with the new Khan Uzbeck, who gave him his sister Kontchaka in marriage, and ordered that George should have possession of Souzdal. He returned to Moscow with a Tartar army and Michael, considering the odds, proposed to cede Vladimir on condition that his own patrimony of Tver should remain intact. George refused, and the war broke out anew. Michael defeated him and captured Kontchaka and the Tartar general, but he released his prisoners, and the dispute was again brought before the khan. George took good care to be at Sarai, and having ample means at his disposal from his poll-tax collecting, distributed bribes right and left. Michael, confident in the justice of his cause, committed the mistake of sending his twelve-year-old son in charge of high boyards, to represent him; but when he was informed of George's methods, he, too, proceeded to Sarai, after making his will. Upon his arrival, he was accused of having drawn his sword upon the Khan's envoy, and of having poisoned Kontchaka. Uzbeck would not even listen to such absurd complaints, but George invented other falsehoods, and at last Michael was arrested. The khan went on a hunting trip in the Caucasus, and the wretched Duke of Tver was dragged after him in chains. One day he was put in the pillory in the market of a populous town, where the people crowded around him to look at the man who, a short time before, was a powerful prince in his own country. Michael's boyards urged him to escape, but he dreaded the khan's vengeance upon his family and people. George increased his bribes, and thus secured the order that Michael should be put to death.

One of Michael's pages came to the tent occupied by him, and told him that George and a Tartar general were approaching. "I know what their object is," said the unfortunate duke. He at once sent his young son to one of the khan's wives, who had promised to protect the child. The two men came to the tent and ordered the Tver boyards to leave. Hired assassins were called in, and a Russian ruffian named Romanetz stabbed the unfortunate duke. When George and the Tartar entered, they saw the nude corpse; it had been despoiled. The Tartar was shocked. "What!" he cried, "Will you allow the body of your uncle to be outraged!" George only smiled; but one of his attendants threw a cloak over the murdered man.

When Michael's children grew up, one of his sons, Dmitri of the Terrible Eyes, secured some friends at the khan's court. He obtained the title of grand duke, and a baskak received orders to install him. When George heard this, he hurried to Sarai; there the two men met, and Dmitri, drawing his sword, killed his father's murderer (1325). Dmitri was arrested and put to death by order of the khan, but his brother Alexander was permitted to succeed him at Tver.

This duke was in sympathy with the people. Suffering under the oppression of the Tartar tax collectors, the people revolted under the leadership of Alexander. The palace of the baskak was attacked, and he and his attendants were killed. Uzbeck, incited by Ivan Kalita, George's brother and successor at Moscow, prepared to take revenge, when Ivan volunteered to punish Tver, as well as Riazan and Novgorod which had given evidence of sympathy. The offer was accepted, and Ivan at the head of a Muscovite army reenforced by 50,000 Tartars marched upon the doomed city. Alexander and his brothers fled. Tver and two other cities were sacked, the Duke of Riazan was put to death, and Novgorod had to pay a heavy fine. Ivan thought that his services would procure him Tver and Riazan, but Uzbeck did not intend to extend the power of the treacherous family, and Constantine, another son of Michael, was made Duke of Tver. He and Ivan went to Sarai, where the latter was ordered to bring Alexander before the khan. The prince had found an asylum in Pskof, where Ivan's messengers appeared to demand his surrender. The envoys urged him to give himself up under the plea "not to expose a Christian people to the wrath of the infidels." The people of Pskof thought otherwise. "Do not go to the Horde, my lord," said they; "whatever happens, we will die with you." Alexander refused to obey the summons, and the people of Pskof began to construct a new fort. Ivan Kalita, the Grand Duke of Moscow, persuaded the Metropolitan to place Alexander and Pskof under the ban of the Church, which was done. We see here a Christian prince persecuting a relative, and a Christian priest excommunicating a Christian people,—all to please an infidel conqueror! Still the people of Pskof refused to yield, but Alexander left the city and took refuge in Lithuania. Then Pskof informed Ivan of his departure, saying, "Alexander is gone; all Pskof swears it, from the smallest to the greatest, popes,[10] monks, nuns, orphans, women, and children." (1329.)

[Footnote 10: Priests.]

Some years afterwards an attempt was made by Alexander to recover Tver. He went to Sarai with some of his boyards. There he made submission. "Lord, all-powerful Czar," he said, "if I have done anything against you, I have come hither to receive of you life or death. Do as God inspires you; I am ready for either." Uzbeck pardoned him and Alexander returned to Tver. This did not please Ivan Kalita, who knew that he was hated everywhere, and that his enemies only needed a leader. He went to Sarai where he told Uzbeck that Alexander was a very dangerous enemy to the Tartars. Alexander was summoned to appear and when he complied, he was arrested, condemned to death, and beheaded.

X

DECLINE OF THE TARTAR POWER
DMITRI DONSKOI

Crafty and unscrupulous, the grand dukes of Moscow were feared by their neighbors. Ivan Kalita, as farmer of the poll-tax, grew immensely wealthy. He collected a double tax from Novgorod, which the republic, although allied with Lithuania, dared not refuse. He bought several towns, besides land in the neighborhood of Vladimir, Rostof, and Kostroma. His title was still Grand Duke of Vladimir, but Moscow was the real capital. Ivan took very good care to stand well with the Church. He built convents and churches, and never went out without an alms-bag or *kalita* to give money to the poor; hence his surname. The seat of the Metropolitan was still at Vladimir, but he often came to Moscow, and finally moved there; so that it became also the capital of the Church. It is reported that the Metropolitan said to Ivan, "God will bless you and raise you above all other dukes, and this city above all other cities. Your house will reign in this place during many centuries; their hands will conquer all their enemies; the saints will make their dwelling here, and here my bones shall rest."

When Ivan with the Alms-bag died in 1341, he left the bulk of his possessions to his eldest son Simeon, and gave only small estates to his other children; he also forbade that Moscow's territory should be divided. His body was scarcely in the grave before the dukes of Tver and Souzdal were on the way to Sarai to claim the grand dukedom of Vladimir; they were supported by other dukes who disliked and dreaded the Muscovite family. Simeon hurried after them, well provided with some of his father's treasure. He used it so well, that he received the iarlikh, and was installed at Vladimir. Servile toward the khan, he was overbearing toward the other Russian dukes, which procured for him the surname of the Proud. He was the first to assume the title of Grand Duke of all the Russias; and, acting in that capacity, he graciously confirmed the charter of Novgorod, for which he demanded and obtained payment. Simeon died in 1353 of the "black death," a pestilence which was imported from Asia.

Great changes were taking place at Sarai, in the Khan of the Golden Horde. Its power was broken by internal discord, when Mourout, the legal heir of Bati, was attacked by a rival Mamai, who succeeded in establishing himself at Sarai. Simeon was succeeded by his brother, Ivan II, an easy-going, good-natured man whose reign of six years did not increase the influence of Moscow. At his death, in 1359, he left several minor children, the oldest of whom was Dmitri, a boy of twelve. Dmitri of Souzdal went to Sarai—and secured the iarlikh, which made him Grand Duke of Vladimir, but Alexis, the Metropolitan, was loyal to Ivan's children, and appealed to the khan in the name of his young ward. Mourout, the heir of Bati, declared in his favor, and young Dmitri was taken to Vladimir escorted by an army, and installed. (1363.)

The appointment was disputed by the dukes of Tver, Souzdal, and Riazan. Dmitri of Souzdal held an iarlikh from Mourout's opponent, and tried to enter in Vladimir, but was expelled. The Metropolitan excommunicated the opponents of Ivan's son, who held the fort as Grand Duke. Young Dmitri made war upon the Duke of Tver, and after a seven years' struggle (1368-1375), compelled him to renounce his claims.

Dmitri was summoned before the Khan, in 1371. He went but what he saw at Sarai convinced him that the Tartars were no longer able to uphold their authority. He did not hesitate to engage in a struggle with Riazan, although it was supported by a Tartar army. Thereafter, when orders arrived from the khan, Dmitri ignored them. In 1376, he sent a large army to Kazan on the Volga, and forced two Mongol chiefs to pay tribute. Two years later, in 1378, a battle was fought between Dmitri and one of Mamai's generals in Riazan, when the Tartars were defeated, which made the grand duke exclaim: "Their time is come, and God is with us!" The khan sent an army to ravage Riazan, and made preparations to reestablish his authority at Moscow.

To make sure of success, Mamai took two years to collect an immense army and to mature his plans. This could not remain secret to the Russians, who, aroused by Dmitri, laid aside their private feuds to make common cause against the infidels. A large number of dukes assembled at Moscow, and even the Lithuanians promised to send troops to Kostroma where the Russian army was gathering. The Metropolitan assured Dmitri of the victory, and sent two monks to go with the troops. Making the sign of the Cross on their cowls, he said, "Behold a weapon which faileth never!"

Russia was united against the Mongol; all the dukes, with the exception of those of Tver and Riazan, lent their aid. These two dreaded Moscow's power, and the Duke of Riazan tried to conclude an alliance with Jagellon of Lithuania and Mamai.

R. Van Bergen

Dmitri, at the head of an army estimated at 150,000 men, marched through Riazan to the Don where the Tartars were drawn up, awaiting the reinforcements of their ally Jagellon, who was still fifteen leagues distant. Dmitri resolved to fight the Tartars before a junction could be effected. He crossed the Don and met the enemy on the plain of Koulikovo,—the Field of the Woodcocks,—where a furious battle was fought. It was decided by a sudden attack upon the Tartars from an ambush, which threw them into a panic. The Tartars were routed; Mamai's camp, his chariots and camels, were all captured. Dmitri was found in a swoon from loss of blood. He was surnamed Donskoi, in honor of this victory. (1380.)

It seemed as if the end of the Mongol yoke had come, when another great leader appeared among them. Tamerlane, after conquering Bokhara, Hindostan, Iran, and Asia Minor, entered Europe, and ordered Mamai to be put to death. He summoned Dmitri Donskoi to appear before him, and received a curt refusal. Tamerlane sent one of his generals with an immense army to Moscow, and Dmitri, not finding the former support, went to Kostroma to collect troops. The Tartars appeared before Moscow, which they tried to carry by assault but failed. They pretended to enter into nego-tiations, when they surprised the gates and Moscow was delivered up to fire and sword. It is said that 24,000 inhabi-tants were slaughtered. Vladimir and other towns suffered the same fate.

It is told that Dmitri wept when he saw the charred remains of his capital after the Tartars had withdrawn. There was nothing for it but to make peace with the khan, and once more the Tartar tax gatherers went their rounds. But Dmitri's heart was sore against the Dukes of Tver and Riazan who had abetted Mamai, and Novgorod, which had used the opportunity of Moscow's distress to plunder some of its towns. After the country had sufficiently recovered, he compelled the Duke of Riazan to conclude "a perpetual peace," and Novgorod paid an indemnity besides agreeing to an annual tribute.

When Dmitri died in 1389, he left Moscow the most powerful of Russian dukedoms. He was succeeded by his eldest son Vassili, with the consent of his cousin Vladimir, who was the eldest of the family. Vassili mentioned Novgorod as "his patrimony," and acted as if the republic was his private property. He visited Sarai in 1392, and while there bought an iarlikh, which placed him in possession of Souzdal, Nishni Novgorod, and Mourom. In 1393, the people of Novgorod revolted, but Vassili's army convinced them that the republic was fast losing its former power.

At this time Tamerlane, dissatisfied with his generals, arrived in Europe and after pillaging the Golden Horde, moved westward, spreading ruin and desolation. He drew near to Moscow, where the famous eikon of the Virgin was taken in solemn procession, when the Tartar army stopped and turned to the south, where Azof, Astrakhan, and Sarai, were plundered and destroyed. (1395.) After Tamerlane's withdrawal, Vassili pretended not to know to whom to pay the tribute,—and so paid none at all. The Tartars under Ediger marched upon Moscow to collect it, but the city was bravely defended and Ediger, fearing an invasion from Asia, agreed to accept a ransom of 3000 rubles, which was paid by the boyards.

More dangerous were the attacks of Vitovt of Lithuania, Vassili's father-in-law, who marched three times against Moscow. Both Vitovt and Vassili were indisposed to risk a decisive battle, fearing that, if defeated, their enemies would despoil them. In 1408 a treaty was signed whereby the Ouger was made the frontier between them. This gave Smolensk to Lithuania, and Kozelsk to Moscow.

Vassili extended his territory, and with it his name; one of his daughters married the Byzantine Emperor, John Palaeologus. At his death, in 1425, he left his territory to his son Vassili, the Blind, whose title was contested by his uncle George, on the ground of being the eldest of the family. The dispute was submitted to the khan, in 1431. Both sides humbled themselves, but the argument of Vassili's boyards prevailed. "My Lord Czar," they said to the khan, "let us speak,—us, the slaves of the grand duke. Our master, the grand duke, prays for the throne of the grand dukedom, which is your property, having no other title but your protection, your investiture, and your iarlikh. You are master and can dispose of it according to your good pleasure. My Lord, the Duke George, his uncle, claims the grand dukedom by the act and will of his father, but not as a favor from the all-powerful." Vassili the Blind, was the first grand duke to be crowned at Moscow instead of at Vladimir.

His reign was disturbed by constant wars with his uncle, and afterwards with his cousins. In 1446 he was taken prisoner by one of the latter, who ordered his eyes to be put out. In 1450, peace was restored when the second son of George died of poison. Notwithstanding the loss of his sight Vassili displayed considerable energy in reestablishing his authority. Novgorod was forced to pay another indemnity, and to give a written promise that in future all deeds would be void unless stamped with the seal of the grand duke.

The most remarkable incident of Vassili's reign was the Council at Florence, Italy, in 1449, where delegates of the Roman and Greek Churches tried to effect a union. There were seventeen Metropolitans, among them Isidore of Moscow, who signed the Act of Union. When Isodore returned and declared what he had done, a great opposition appeared. Vassili himself insulted the Metropolitan, who fled to Rome. In 1453, Mahomet II captured Constantinople when a host of priests, monks, artists, and learned men fled from the extinct Byzantine Empire, to find an asylum in Russia.

While nothing resulted from the Council of Florence, owing to the opposition of members of the Greek Church, the fall of Constantinople left a deep impression upon Russia, which chose to consider itself as the heir to the Byzantine Empire. More than this, the influence of the men who found a refuge in Russia, served to inoculate the country of their adoption with the semi-oriental civilization which had distinguished Constantinople from Western Europe. The time, too, was propitious. Russia was gradually recovering from the blow of Tartar rule, which had marred its progress during two centuries. Here was, therefore, to all intent and purposes, a virgin soil, which promised to yield a rich harvest to whatever principles were planted in it. It might even regenerate the decaying elements of the Byzantine civilization.

R. Van Bergen

XI

IVAN III, THE GREAT

Vassili's eldest son Ivan was born in 1440. It is said that upon the occasion of his birth, an old monk at Novgorod had a vision which he reported to the Archbishop. "Truly," he said, "it is to-day that the grand duke triumphs; God has given him an heir; I behold this child making himself illustrious by glorious deeds. He will subdue princes and nations. But woe to Novgorod! Novgorod will fall at his feet, and never rise again."

Vassili, wishing to avoid the disputes incident upon the succession, during his lifetime admitted Ivan as co-regent. Upon his father's death, in 1462, Ivan was twenty-two years old. He succeeded without the usual disturbances, and the first six years of his reign were uneventful. In 1468, he gained forcible possession of his brother George's estate, and allowed him to die in prison. When he heard of his death,—he wept. Another brother, Andrew, was in his way, and was flung into prison, whereupon Ivan called the Metropolitan and bishops to his palace, wept some more, and confessed that he had been too severe;—but he forgot to restore Andrew's property. When his third brother, Boris, died, Ivan seized the estate and kept it; but he wept some more.

This soft-hearted but tenacious gentleman found fault with his neighbor, Michael of Tver, for entering into an alliance with Lithuania. To settle the difficulty, he invaded the dukedom, and annexed it to Moscow. Then, having his hands free, he thought of Novgorod. The Germans of the Hanseatic League had formed a colony in the old republic, which had grown very wealthy. Ivan looked upon that wealth as his; if it was not, it ought to be. Acting upon this satisfactory conclusion, he remembered that the people of Novgorod had omitted to do him homage when he succeeded his father. They had even failed to appreciate the gentle letter of remonstrance in which he reminded them of their oversight. Good-natured as he knew himself to be, he could not afford to encourage such a rebellious spirit; but, being a careful man, he concluded that it would be more humane as well as cheaper to try the gentle means of bribery. His gold, distributed where it would do most good, procured him a large party. The opposition was led by a woman named Marfa, the wealthy widow of a possadnik. She urged that the republic should ask the help of Casimir IV, King of Poland, but Ivan's friends in the vetche replied that, if Poland should win, the Roman Catholic Church would enter, whereas Russia was at least loyal to the Greek Church.

Marfa's influence prevailed; the republic submitted to Poland, on condition that its charter should be respected. Gentle Ivan despatched some Envoys to warn the people of the error of their ways, and when that did no good, he hired Tartar cavalry, overran the territory of the republic, and directed his troops to cut off the noses and lips of the prisoners. It is probable that he wept, although history omits mentioning the fact. Novgorod was unprepared; a mob was collected and styled an army, and in the battle of the Chelona, 3,000 trained troops put to flight 30,000 citizen soldiers. Novgorod was lost. Ivan kindly permitted the name "republic" to continue, but his authority was admitted. He also received a share of the wealth as an indemnity. (1470.)

Two years later he married the niece and supposed heiress of the last Byzantine emperor. Her father, Thomas Palaeologus, had fled to Rome where he died leaving one daughter Sophia. Pope Paul II wished to find her a husband, and Cardinal Bessarion of the Greek Church advised him to offer her hand to Ivan. The offer was accepted; Sophia received a dower from the Pope who still hoped to unite the two churches, and the bride was received with great honor in Ivan's territory. The grand duke probably had his eye on Constantinople, but deferred his claim to some favorable opportunity. With Sophia came many Greek nobles, artists, and learned men. Ivan, as may be judged from his gentle nature, was a patron of art, and had no prejudice against foreigners. Several Italians came to Moscow where their services were appreciated.

Ivan left Novgorod in peace during five years, when he thought it time to familiarize the citizens with the fact that their republic was a thing of the past. He needed a pretext; by a judicious use of money, his agents raised a mob against the boyards, who, being assaulted, invoked the strong arm of the law, in the person of Ivan. The grand duke came to Novgorod in 1475, to hold court. He at once ordered the arrest of the possadnik, Marfa's son, and a number of boyards who believed in a republic, had them put in chains and carried to Moscow. This was in violation of the charter, but Ivan had an elastic conscience. Next he tempted a scribe to mention him as *Sovereign* instead of "lord," in an official document; and when, in a last effort to save the republic, Marfa's partisans killed a number of Ivan's friends, it was evidently his duty to restore order.

Upon his return to Moscow, he announced that Novgorod was the enemy of the Greek Church, and the ally of the Pope and of Lithuania. This so alarmed the Metropolitan and the priests that they begged Ivan to make war upon the wicked city. Many dukes and boyards, moved by loyalty for the church, and perhaps scenting spoils, flocked to his camp. Marfa's partisans in vain tried to arouse the citizens by the cry, "Let us die for liberty and St. Sophia!" It fell on deaf ears; every one for himself, was the general thought. Novgorod surrendered. Ivan guaranteed,—for just so long as it should suit him,—the people's lives and property, their ancient code of laws, and exemption from Muscovite service; but the vetche and office of possadnik were abolished, and with them died the republic. (1478.)

Having settled with Novgorod to his satisfaction, Ivan bethought himself of establishing peace in his own household. Russian writers state that his wife, Sophia, annoyed him by often repeating the interesting inquiry, "How long am I to be the slave of the Tartars?" The Khan of the Golden Horde had been dissolved since Tamerlane's raid; several states had been formed from it, of which the principal were Kazan, Sarai or Astrakhan, and the Crimea. Kazan was ruled by a czar; its people were the descendants of Mongols and Bulgars who had made great progress in commerce. The Khan of Sarai and his men clung to the life of nomads; but the subjects of the Khan of the Crimea, were Mongols, Armenians, Greeks, Jews, and Italians; and all three had this in common that they were constantly indulging in quarrels and strife at home.

Ivan knew all this, because sometimes a chief would come to Moscow for an asylum, and others took service in his army. He no longer sent tribute, although occasionally, when he was occupied elsewhere, he did send a small present. In 1478 Khan Akhmet sent ambassadors to Moscow to remind him that the tribute was in arrears. Ivan, who had apparently a wonderful command over his features, pretended to lose his temper, jumped on the picture of the khan, and ordered all the envoys except one to be put to death. The survivor was told to go home, and tell his master of his reception.

Ivan had reasonable cause for thinking that Akhmet would be displeased, and collected an army of 150,000 men on the Oka, where he took up a strong position. He had been right in his conjecture, for Akhmet gathered an army and in due time arrived on the opposite bank of the river. Ivan had time to reflect. He did not much fancy risking a decisive battle, and returned to Moscow to consult his mother, the boyards, and the priests. All urged him to fight, and finally he came back to the camp, convinced that scheming and plotting were more in his line. All this time the two armies lay within earshot, exchanging complimentary remarks, with no casualties. The khan offered to pardon Ivan on condition that he should come and hold his stirrup; or, if he were too tired, if he should send some high officer to do it in his name. Ivan shook his head. Meanwhile the priests at Moscow were growing impatient, and the Archbishop Vassian sent him a warm letter. It happened that Akhmet was quite as prudent as Ivan; but when the winter came and the Oka, instead of a barrier, became an easy crossing, Ivan ordered the retreat. Just then the two armies, led by such brave commanders, were seized with a panic, and away they fled in opposite directions. (1480.) The honors were with Ivan, because he did not have so far to run as Akhmet, who did not stop until he reached Sarai. It is not stated why Ivan received no surname from this great battle.

The following year, 1481, Ivan had sufficiently recovered to show the courage he possessed. There was a disturbance in Novgorod, where the people did not appreciate the nobility of his character. He ordered some of the boyards to be tortured and put to death, and *eight thousand* citizens were forcibly packed off to Souzdal.

In fear of his doughty enemy Akhmet, Ivan made friends with the Khan of the Crimea, calculating that if the former should attack him again, he would have to look out for his rear. Akhmet, however, seemed to have had enough of it, and Ivan, who was on bad terms with Lithuania and Poland, suggested to his friend that a raid into those territories might pay. The Khan of the Crimea took the hint; he penetrated as far as Kief which he captured and pillaged. (1482.) The famous monastery of the Catacombs was almost destroyed; but Ivan had the satisfaction of knowing that his two enemies had other things to think of, instead of annoying him.

In 1487 war broke out with Kazan. A Russian army marched against it, but Ivan did not take command. As a result, the city was taken and the khan, who had assumed the title of czar, was brought a prisoner to Moscow. Fearing that he would unite the other Tartars against him if he annexed the territory at once, he appointed a nephew of his friend, the Khan of the Crimea, but placed Russian soldiers in the fortress, while he added the title of Prince of Bulgaria to his own. Other Tartar princes sent envoys to protest against the arrest. Ivan did not receive them in person, and refused to release the prisoner, but he ordered the envoys to be treated with great honor and gave them so many presents, that they returned in great good humor.

In 1492, the King of Poland died, leaving that kingdom to his eldest son Albert, and Lithuania to his second son Alexander. Ivan was justly indignant that he had not been remembered in the will. He sent envoys to Bajazet II, Sultan of Turkey, to the Kings of Hungary and Moldavia, and to his old friend the Khan of the Crimea, to secure their assistance or at least their kind neutrality. Of the services of the Khan of the Crimea he felt assured.

He began by discovering a Polish plot against his life at

Moscow, and appealed to the religious prejudices of the Lithuanian nobles belonging to the Greek Church, omitting to mention his little arrangement with the infidel sultan. When Alexander sent envoys to negotiate terms of peace, Ivan's deputies said to them: "Lithuania has profited by the misfortunes of Russia to take our territory, but to-day things are changed." They were right. When peace was concluded in 1494, Ivan's frontier in the west was extended.

The marriage of Alexander to Ivan's daughter seemed to end the hostility between the two countries, but nothing was further from the schemes of the wily grand duke. He stipulated that she should have a Greek chapel in the palace, and warned her never to appear in a Catholic church, and always to wear the Russian national dress. Soon after the wedding Ivan complained that his daughter was forced to wear Polish costumes, and that the Greek Church was being persecuted. These were to him ample cause for war, the more so since he had good reason to count upon his friends, the priests and boyards of the Greek Church. When the war broke out, cities where the majority of the people belonged to that church, opened their gates to his army, and Alexander was badly defeated in the battle of Vedrocha. This war added another slice to Ivan's territory.

Alexander in his distress made an alliance with the Livonian Order and with the Great Horde at Sarai; but Ivan's old friend, the Khan of the Crimea, made a raid in Gallicia and Volhynia, and the Lithuanians were defeated at Mstislaf; but they compelled the Russians to raise the siege of Smolensk. Meanwhile Ivan had serious trouble. In 1495, he ordered the merchants of several Hanseatic towns to be arrested at Novgorod, and incidentally had goods to the value of $200,000,—an immense sum in those days,—carried to Moscow. This caused the foreign merchants to leave for safer places; but the Livonian Order invaded his territory, and in the battle of Siritza, they crushed a Russian army of 50,000 men, but the following year, 1502, they were defeated at Pskof.

Toward the end of his life he was in doubt about his successor, because his eldest son was dead. At first he thought of making his grandson Dmitri, his heir; but he changed his mind, sent his daughter-in-law and grandson to prison and proclaimed his second son Vassili his heir. He died in 1505, after a reign of forty-three years. It was under his direction that a new code of laws, the Oulogenia, was prepared.

XII

RUSSIA BECOMES AN AUTOCRACY

Vassili, Ivan's son, showed a great resemblance to his father. He did not evince any greater love for his near relatives, as one of his first acts was to put his nephew Dmitri in prison, where he died. One of his brothers who did not like his manners, tried to escape, but was brought back and severely punished.

The republic of Pskof, and the dukedoms of Riazan and Novgorod-Seversky were still enjoying some degree of liberty, which Vassili did not approve. At Pskof, the grand duke was represented by *a namiestnik*, or ducal delegate; the people, citizens and peasants, nobles and lower classes, quarreled constantly among themselves, but united to quarrel with the delegate. Vassili determined to put an end to this. He came to Novgorod to hold court, and summoned the magistrates of Pskof to appear before him, and when they arrived he ordered their arrest. A merchant of Pskof heard of it and, hurrying home, told the people. Immediately the bell was rung to convoke the vetche, and the masses called for war with Moscow. More prudent counsels prevailed when messengers arrived from the prisoners, imploring their friends not to try a useless resistance and to avoid the shedding of blood. A leading citizen was sent to Vassili to offer him submission; he was dismissed with the answer that one of the *diaks* or secretaries would come to Pskof to let the people know the terms. When that officer arrived, he was admitted in the vetche, where he informed his hearers that Vassili imposed two conditions, namely, that Pskof and the towns subject to it must receive his delegates, and that the vetche must be abolished and the great bell, used to convoke it, must be taken down. Twenty-four hours were asked to deliberate. Before the time expired, the vetche met for the last time, when the first magistrate addressed the delegate. "It is written in our chronicles," he said, "that our ancestors took oaths to the grand duke. The people of Pskof swore never to rebel against our lord who is at Moscow, nor to ally themselves with Lithuania, with Poland, nor with the Germans, otherwise the wrath of God would be upon them, bringing with it famine, fires, floods, and the invasion of the infidels. If the grand duke, on his part, did not observe his vow, he dared the same consequences. Now our town and our bell are in the power of God and the duke. As for us, we have kept our oath." The great bell was taken to Novgorod, and Vassili visited "his patrimony." Three hundred wealthy families were transported to other cities and replaced by as many families from Moscow. When he departed from Pskof, he left a garrison of 5,000 guards and 500 artillerymen. That was the end of the last republic in Russia. (1510.)

In 1521, it was the turn of Riazan whose duke was accused of having entered into an alliance with the Khan of the Crimea. He was summoned to Moscow, where he was arrested, but he managed to escape. His dukedom, however, was annexed to Moscow. Two years later, in 1523, the Duke of Novgorod-Severski was put in prison for underhand dealing with Poland, and that dukedom was added to Vassili's territories. This rounded up Vassili's possessions in Central Russia.

The grand duke continued his father's policy toward Lithuania. When Alexander died, he tried to become Grand Duke of Wilna, but the King of Poland was too quick for him. War broke out, but neither gained any important advantage, and in 1509 a *perpetual peace* was concluded wherein Vassili renounced all claims upon Kief and Smolensk. The "perpetual peace" lasted three years. Vassili then went to the other extreme, by declaring that "as long as his horse was in marching condition and his sword cut sharp, there should be neither peace nor truce with Lithuania." In 1514, the Russian army besieged and took Smolensk, but in the same year they were badly defeated in the battle of Orcha.

The two grand dukes tried to involve as many allies as they could. The Khan of the Crimea, the useful friend of Vassili's father, had become the son's enemy; Vassili offset him by an alliance with the Khan of Astrakhan. When Sigismund tried to secure the help of Sweden, Vassili sought that of Denmark; and when his enemy set the Dnieper Cossacks at him, the grand duke induced the Teutonic Order to invade Poland. After Sigismund was defeated at Smolensk, the Emperor of Germany and the Pope offered to mediate; the latter advised Vassili to let Lithuania alone, and to turn his attention toward Constantinople. Negotiations commenced in 1520, but it was six years later before a truce was concluded. On this occasion Vassili made a speech in which he praised Emperor Charles V, and Pope Clement VII,—but Lithuania lost Smolensk. It was during this war that the partition of Poland was first mentioned.

Vassili did not neglect the east, even while engaged in the west. Kazan had expelled the nephew of the Khan of the Crimea whom Ivan III had appointed, and elected a Khan hostile to Russia. Two expeditions were sent against the city but nothing was effected. When this khan died, Vassili succeeded in installing a friendly prince, but he was overthrown and a relative of the Khan of the Crimea took his place. He prepared a great invasion of Russia in 1521, and did gain a decided victory on the Oka, after which he ravaged the territory of the grand duke. Vassili was compelled to humble himself before the khan, in order to save Moscow; he made him presents and in the treaty signed by him, called himself the khan's tributary. When the khan withdrew, he was attacked in Riazan and the treaty was taken away from him. The invasion was, however, a calamity for the grand dukedom, which was devastated by fire, and a host of women and children were carried off, to be sold as slaves at Astrakhan and Kaffa.

The following year Vassili collected a large army on the Oka and challenged the Khan of the Crimea to come and give battle. The offer was declined with the remark that he knew the way into Russia, and that he was not in the habit of consulting his enemies as to when and where he was to fight.

Hoping to profit by the quarrels among the Tartars, Vassili sent an expedition to Kazan in 1523, and again in 1524, but both were unsuccessful. Kazan owed its wealth to a fair, which attracted a host of merchants. Vassili thought that he would destroy his enemy's prosperity by establishing a rival fair. Accordingly one was opened at Makarief, and this time the grand duke's expectations were realized. This was the origin of the world-famous fair at Nishni Novgorod, whither it was transferred afterwards.

Vassili made a long stride forward in the direction of autocracy. He consulted neither boyard nor priest. He deposed the Metropolitan and banished him to a monastery. Prince Kholmski, who was married to one of Vassili's sisters, was thrown into prison for failing to show abject respect. When one of the boyards complained that "The grand duke decided all the questions, shut up with two others in the bedchamber," the noble was promptly arrested, condemned to death, and executed. He interrupted the objection of a high noble with, "Be silent, lout!" His court displayed great splendor, but it was semi-Asiatic. The throne was guarded by young nobles called *ryndis*, dressed in long caftans of white satin, high caps of white fur, and carrying silver hatchets.

Like his father, he tried to attract artists and learned men, and exchanged embassies with most of the European Courts. He extended the frontiers of his empire, but ruthlessly suppressed free thought. It has been claimed that the Slav is fit only for an absolute government. The history of Russia contradicts the statement. The idea of autocracy was Asiatic and was imported with the Tartar yoke.

XIII

IVAN IV, THE TERRIBLE

When Vassili died in 1533, he left two infant sons, Ivan and George, the elder three years old. His widow, Helena Glinski, assumed the regency. She was a woman remarkable for spirit and beauty, and showed her courage in ruthlessly suppressing every attempt of high nobles to contest her authority. She sent her husband's brother George to prison, and let him die there. One of her own uncles, who had been in her confidence, showed too much ambition and suffered the same fate. Andrew, another brother of Vassili, tried to make his escape; he was promptly brought back and placed in confinement. This caused an unimportant war with Poland, ending in a truce in 1537. The Tartars of Kazan and the Crimea were frequently defeated. But Helena was cordially hated by the great nobles at Moscow; she was poisoned, and died in 1538.

Ivan, the oldest son and heir, was then eight years old. It must be placed to the credit of his mother that he had learned to read, for the children were sadly neglected after her death, and it was the boy's principal solace and occupation. In later years Ivan wrote of this time, "We and our brother Iouri (George) were treated like strangers, like the children of beggars. We were ill-clothed, cold and hungry." What impressed the child especially, was that when foreign envoys arrived he was placed upon the throne and the same nobles who showed him such contemptuous indifference, were respectful and even servile on such occasions. He noticed, too, that when these proud nobles needed anything, it was necessary that the papers should be signed by him. All this set the child thinking, and being a manly, bright boy, he came to the conclusion that, after all, he was the real master.

After many quarrels among themselves, Andrew Chouiski, the head of a noble family, had become all-powerful; all important offices were occupied by his favorites and friends. Ivan noticed it all, but said nothing. He was thirteen years old when, after the Christmas celebration of 1543, he suddenly summoned the boyards before him, and in a threatening tone sternly accused them of their misdeeds. "There are among you many guilty ones," he said, "but this time I am satisfied with making one example." He ordered the guards to seize Andrew Chouiski, and had him then and there torn to pieces by dogs. After this terrible punishment, he ordered the arrest of the most disobedient nobles, who were transported to distant places.

The thirteen-year-old boy then assumed the government, relying chiefly upon his mother's relations, the Glinskis. In 1547, at the age of seventeen, he directed the Metropolitan to crown him, not as Grand Duke but as Czar. In a Bible printed in the Slavonic language, he had read of the *Czar* Nebuchadnezzar, the *Czar* Pharaoh, David, *Czar* of Israel, etc. He knew, besides, that the former masters of the grand dukes, the khans, had been addressed by that title. Perhaps it was because he wished it to be known that he considered himself the equal of any Tartar ruler; perhaps because he desired to have a title superior to that of the nobles who descended from former grand dukes, and who inherited the rank without the power; at any rate Ivan IV was crowned as the first Czar.

Young as he was, and since his thirteenth year beyond control, Ivan's life had been the reverse of good. But when, soon after the coronation, he married Anastasia Romanof, he made an earnest effort to reform. The relatives of his mother and of his wife, the Glinskis and the Romanofs, enjoyed his favor at this time.

There was much suppressed dissatisfaction among the nobles, and many plots were hatched against him. In the year of his coronation, a fire swept wooden Moscow, and about 1,700 people perished in the flames. Ivan ordered an investigation, and withdrew to Vorobief. Crowds gathered in the thoroughfares, when mysterious persons appeared among them declaring that the Glinskis had set the city on fire. Soon after shouts were heard, "It is the Princess Anne Glinski who, with her two sons, has bewitched the city; she has taken human hearts, plunged them in water, and with this water has sprinkled the houses. This is the cause of the destruction of Moscow!" A mob collected and made for the palace of the Glinskis and one of them, George, was stabbed. They went on to Vorobief, where they demanded the life of Ivan's uncle. The czar's own life was in danger and the mob had to be dispersed by force.

Ivan did not forget this, and terrible was his vengeance upon the boyards. At this time he gave his confidence to two men, one a priest named Silvester, who had the reputation of being a very honest man; the other, a member of the smaller nobility, named Adachef who, in 1551, as Minister of the Interior, gave to Russian cities the first municipal liberties. Ivan showed an unusual interest in the people; it was under his orders that a new code of laws (Soudebnik) was prepared, and many reforms were made in the Church.

This rather increased than diminished the hostility of the nobles. Ivan's favorites, Silvester and Adachef had grown ambitious and the former especially was overbearing. He openly opposed the czar, and tried to sow discord between him and his wife. When Ivan's favorite son died, Silvester told him that it was a punishment from heaven for his disobedience. The two men tried to procure the dismissal of the Glinskis and Romanofs, and for that purpose made friends with the boyards whom Ivan suspected. In 1553, the czar fell dangerously ill; he called in the boyards and ordered them to swear loyalty to his infant son Dmitri. They refused. He was informed that the nobles were conspiring with his cousin Vladimir, whose mother was distributing money in the army. He was in terror for the lives of his wife and son. Once he said to the boyards who had remained faithful, "Do not, I pray you, forget that you have sworn an oath to my son and to me; do not let him fall into the hands of the boyards; fly with him to some foreign country, whithersoever God may guide you." Ivan recovered but he never could forget the anguish of those days.

Ivan's character at this time was far from bad. He was only twenty years old, and on several occasions showed that he was compassionate instead of cruel. It was only natural that his nature should be perverted, surrounded as he was by men of whom he was suspicious. Still, such a change could only be gradual. The immediate consequence of the conduct of his nobles, was that it drew him closer to the people. This was shown in 1506, when he convoked the three orders, nobles, priests, and people, to discuss public affairs.

His first act, after his recovery, was to banish his former favorites. Silvester was ordered to the monastery of St. Cyril, and Adachef was sent to Livonia. Soon afterwards the Czarina Anastasia died; there was a strong suspicion that she had been poisoned. To add to his bitterness, Prince Andrew

Kourbski, a descendant of Rurik and a great friend of Silvester and Adachef, permitted 15,000 Russians to be defeated by the Poles with whom Ivan was at war. Kourbski deserted to the King of Poland.

It appears that Ivan at this time feared for his life, for he withdrew to a neighboring castle with his friends, servants, and treasures. From there he wrote his abdication in two letters, one addressed to the Metropolitan, the other to the people of Moscow. This action struck terror among the nobles and the people. The former dreaded that the people might rise and avenge the czar, and the people were afraid that the nobles would once again usurp the government. The nobles and priests consulted and decided to beg Ivan's pardon and to submit to any punishment he might impose. Ivan consented to return to Moscow but on his own terms. This was accepted. After his arrival in the capital he established a special guard of one thousand men who had a dog's head and a broom hanging from their saddles, to show that they were ready to bite and ready to sweep the czar's enemies from off Russian soil.

It was then that Ivan began to earn the surname of The Terrible, which has clung to him ever afterwards. We have his own record in a letter to the Monastery of St. Cyril, in which he asks the prayers of the Church for the victims of his vengeance. He appears to have kept a careful account, as we read, "Kazarine Doubrofsky and his two sons, with ten men who came to their assistance;" "Twenty men of the village of Kolmenskoe;" "Eighty of Matveiche." It amazes us to read, "Remember, Lord, the souls of thy servants, to the number of 1,505 persons, Novgorodians." The boyards lived in a state of terror; few among them knew how long they would keep their heads on their shoulders. Neither rank nor title was a safeguard. The Archbishop of Moscow was dismissed, and probably murdered. Alexander, George's widow, and Ivan's sister-in-law, went to the scaffold. Prince Vladimir and his mother, Ivan's uncle and grand-aunt, were also executed. It was on this occasion that the "Novgorodians, to the number of 1,505 persons" were put to death, because Ivan suspected them of a plot to open the gates to the King of Poland. In 1571, there was another wholesale execution, in which several of Ivan's latest favorites were victims.

The burden of his wrath fell upon the boyards. It may have been for the purpose of humiliating them and the Churchmen that he assembled delegates of those two classes to confer with representatives of the merchants of Moscow and Smolensk, about the war with Poland. Ivan addressed the assembly in person, and it was decided that the war should continue.

It was under his reign that British traders accidentally discovered the White Sea and the mouth of the Dwina. They came overland to Moscow where they were well received and secured several privileges. Ivan was anxious to conclude an offensive-defensive alliance with Elizabeth of England, and proposed an agreement to furnish each other with an asylum if either of them should be compelled to fly from the country through being defeated by an enemy or the rebellion of their subjects. Elizabeth did not fancy such an alliance, and declined the offer of an asylum, "finding," as she declared, "by the grace of God no dangers of the sort in her dominions." Ivan never ceased recurring to, and pleading for, such an agreement, thus showing his ever present suspicions.

After commercial intercourse was established with England, and British traders settled in Moscow, Ivan continued to show them his favor. He was himself the greatest merchant of Russia. The furs which he received from Siberia were sold to the foreign merchants at the fairs. His agents went into the provinces where they compelled the people to sell him furs, wax, honey, etc., at such prices as he chose to pay, and the foreign merchants had to buy them from him at a high price. He also bought the imported goods and sold them to Russian merchants. They were not permitted to buy from anybody else, until the goods of the czar were sold.

At the beginning of his reign, in 1551, Ivan was preparing an expedition to Kazan, and in June of the following year he descended the Volga and laid siege to that city. It was captured after a brave defense, when a number of the people were massacred and the rest sold as slaves. This conquest was followed by that of Astrakhan in 1554; the Volga from its source to its mouth was thereafter a Russian river. The Cossacks of the Don also submitted to him.

The European countries bordering on Russia dreaded that country's growing power. Ivan, after his coronation, sent to western Europe to engage a number of engineers and mechanics; these men were stopped on the road, and none of them ever reached Moscow. Sigismund of Poland even threatened to kill the British merchants on the Baltic, "because," he said, "if the Muscovite, who is not only our present adversary, but the eternal enemy of all free countries, should provide himself with guns, bullets, and munitions; and, above all, with mechanics who continue to make arms, hitherto unknown in this barbaric country, he would be a menace to Europe." Ivan, on the other hand, was equally anxious that the Russians should possess all the advantages of Europe's superior civilization. This, added to the inherited hostility between the two countries, caused many wars.

While Ivan was pursuing his conquests in the south, he was attacked by Gustavus Wasa, Sweden's famous king, who entertained the same fears as the King of Poland. The war ended by a commercial treaty whereby Swedish merchants might trade with India and China by way of Russia, and those of Russia with Holland, England, and France by way of Sweden. This war had scarcely ceased before envoys of the Livonian Order arrived to request a renewal of the truce. Ivan demanded tribute for Iourief which he claimed as his "patrimony." This was refused, and war was declared. It was owing to Ivan that this brotherhood was dissolved and its territory divided. In 1566, a truce was proposed by Poland.

It was on this occasion that he called the assembly referred to on page 116. The war continued. Ivan was attacked also by Sultan Selim II of Turkey, in 1569, and the Khan of the Crimea marched straight upon Moscow, set fire to the suburbs, and destroyed the capital except the Kremlin. He carried off a hundred thousand prisoners. (1571.) As he withdrew, he wrote to Ivan: "I burn, I ravage everything on account of Kazan and Astrakhan. I came to you and burned Moscow. I wished to have your crown and your head, but you did not show yourself; you declined a battle and you dare call yourself a Czar of Moscow! Will you live at peace with me? Yield me up Kazan and Astrakhan. If you have only money to offer me, it will be useless were it the riches of the world. What I want is Kazan and Astrakhan! As to the roads to your empire, I have seen them—I know them." The khan made another invasion the next year, 1572, but was defeated.

In the same year Sigismund Augustus II of Poland died. There was a party at Warsaw that proposed to elect Ivan's son, but the czar wanted Poland for himself. He failed in the attempt, and the Duke of Anjou, brother of the King of France, was chosen. He did not like the people and fled; his place was filled by Stephen Batory, Governor of Transsylvania, a young, capable, and energetic noble. Batory took in his service a number of trained German and Hungarian soldiers, and took Polotsk after a brave defense.

He also captured several other towns, but was repulsed at Pskof.

Ivan sought the mediation of Pope Gregory XIII, and a truce was concluded in 1582; Ivan ceded Polotsk and all Livonia.

Ivan, in his manhood, was a man of violent temper. He was never seen without an iron-tipped staff, which he used freely and recklessly upon the people around him. Nobody, whatever his rank, was safe from corporal punishment. He killed his eldest son Ivan with a blow, and suffered from remorse ever afterward. He left a lasting impression upon Russia by his reforms. He made a law whereby neither church nor convents could acquire new lands. He was wonderfully well educated, considering the neglect of his early youth, and tolerant of religious opinions. A Presbyterian and a Lutheran church were built at Moscow with his consent, but in deference to the opposition of the people, they were removed to the suburbs. He was also the founder of the *streltsi* or national guard.

Ivan died in 1584, after a reign of forty-one years.

XIV

RUSSIA UNDER IVAN THE TERRIBLE

The reign of Ivan the Terrible is remarkable, first, because it is the beginning of Russia as we know it in our time; and also because it occurred at a time when Great Britain was exploring the Atlantic, and preparing the way for the wonderful expansion of the English-speaking race, which culminated in the great North American Republic. It was under this reign, in 1558, that Russia's invasion of Asia began, and with it a movement eastward, which has not yet ceased.

It is interesting, therefore, to study the condition of the Russian people at this important period. Although, as we have seen, the Tartar yoke did not influence the people directly, because there was no intercourse between victor and vanquished, the indirect influence was great, owing to the adoption of Tartar habits or customs by the dukes and nobles, during their visits to the khan. During this time intercourse with Europe ceased; hence, in the 16th and 17th centuries, Russia was more Asiatic than European, although the Russians hated the victors. Who can say how much influence this has exerted upon Russia's conquests in Asia?

Among the old Slavs, the family was the unit from which the

State was built up, and this was confirmed under the Tartar yoke. There is some similarity between the Empire of Russia and that of China, for there, too, the family is the unit. In both countries the Emperor is not only the master, he is also considered as the father and high priest of his people. Their persons and property are the emperor's, to do with as he pleases. But in Russia there was a nobility descended from the former dukes; in China there was none, except the descendant of Confucius. Yet in Russia these lords, many of whom traced their descent to Rurik, became in time the slaves of the czar. They prostrated themselves before him, as they had seen the courtiers of the khan do. When they presented a petition, they expressed it by the word *tchelobitie*, which means "beating of the forehead," showing that they performed what is known in China as the *kowtow*. In addressing the czar, they said, "Order me not to be chastised; order me to speak a word!" The Grand Dukes of Moscow considered their territory and the people on it, as their own private property. They had learned this from the khans. The palace, a mixture of oriental splendor and barbarism, showed the influence of the Tartars.

The people of Russia were divided into classes, the lowest of which were the slaves or *kholop*, prisoners of war, men who had sold themselves, or who were born in slavery. Above them were the peasants, born on the estate of a noble, but still known as free men. Then came the peasants who farmed the land of an owner, but these were few. Much of the land was owned by the several mirs or villages, but in the course of time they were assigned to gentlemen, who were able to serve in the army without pay, being supported by the revenues derived from these villages. Gradually these gentlemen looked upon the land of the mir as their own property, but the peasants never did lose the conviction that the mir was the real proprietor. In Ivan's time and later, the mir and not the individual, was held responsible for the tax to the czar, for the free labor furnished to the lord, and for his dues. The mir, therefore, was absolute master over every inhabitant of the village, and this power was vested in the *starost*. The peasant gradually descended into a beast of burden, who was not even a human being, but merely a productive force for the benefit of the State and of the lord.

A Russian town consisted, first of the *kremlin*, a fortress of wood which, when required, was defended by "men of the service"; then came the suburbs, built around the kremlin, and inhabited by the people. They were governed by a *voievod* or governor, appointed by the czar, or by a starost or mayor, elected by the nobles, priests, and privileged citizens. The principal duty of the citizens was to pay the taxes, and therefore they were forbidden to leave the city. Under the Czar Alexis, the penalty for such offense was death.

The merchants did not form a separate class. They are known in Russian as *gosti* or guests, thus showing that, notwith-standing the old and honorable record of Novgorod and Kief, the Tartar yoke and subsequent arbitrary rule of the grand dukes had ruined trade or left it in the hands of aliens. Ivan the Terrible called them the moujiks of commerce. Fletcher, an Englishman who spent many years in Moscow under Ivan IV, gives the following curious pen picture: "Often you will see them trembling with fear, lest a boyard should know what they have to sell. I have seen them at times, when they had spread out their wares so that you might make a better choice, look all around them,—as if they feared an enemy would surprise them and lay hands on them. If I asked them the cause, they would say to me, 'I was afraid that there might be a noble or one of the sons of boyards here: they would take away my merchandise by force.'"

The Russian women were kept secluded in women's quarters as they are in China, but they remained a member of their own family. A wife's duty was "to obey her husband as the slave obeys his master," and she was taught to think of herself as her master's property. He had the right to punish her as he did his children or his slaves. The priest Silvester advises the husband not to use sticks that are too thick or tipped with iron, nor to whip her before his men, but to correct her moderately and in private. No Russian woman dared object to being beaten. A Russian proverb says: "I love you like my soul, and I dust you like my jacket."

The men wore oriental tunics or robes, and a long beard; the women painted their faces. Ivan the Terrible said that to shave the beard was "a sin that the blood of all the martyrs could not cleanse. Was it not to defile the image of man created by God?"

There was a general belief in magic and witchcraft; sorcerers were burned alive in a cage. Ivan, although in advance of his age, was not free from superstition. The art of medicine was, of course, still in its infancy, and those who practiced it were in constant danger of their lives, because if they did not cure a patient, they might suffer for it.

Both the nobles and the people were addicted to the vice of drunkenness. No one paid any attention when a person, rich or poor, young or old, fell down in the street from the effects of drink. This is what the priests said of this vice: "My brethren, what is worse than drunkenness? You lose memory and reason like a madman who does not know what he is doing. The drunkard is senseless; he lies like a corpse. If you speak to him he does not answer. Think of his poor soul which grows foul in its vile body which is its prison.... To drink is lawful and is to the glory of God, who has given us wine to make us rejoice."

The Metropolitan of Moscow, until a Patriarch was

appointed, was supposed to be the head of the Church, but the czar held the real power. There were two classes of priests: The Black Clergy lived as monks in monasteries, some of which were exceedingly wealthy; they were forbidden to marry, and the bishops were appointed from among them. The White Clergy lived among the people and were compelled to marry. Most of them were grossly ignorant. The same Englishman quoted before, Mr. Fletcher, says of these priests: "As for exhorting or instructing their flock, they have neither the habit of it nor the talent for it, for all the clergy are as profoundly ignorant of the Word of God as of all other learning."

The revenues of the Empire consisted of a tax on every sixty measures of corn; of a house-tax, or tax on every fire; the customhouse dues, and what remained of the municipal taxes after paying expenses; of a tax on public baths; the farming out of lands belonging to the crown; the fines and confiscations in the "Court of the Brigands;" and finally of the tribute paid by thirty-six towns and their landed possessions "belonging to the Crown."

The Courts of Justice belonged to the Middle Ages; tortures were applied similar to those employed by the Spanish Inquisition. A wife who murdered her husband "was buried alive up to her neck." Heretics were burned at the stake; sorcerers were burned in an iron cage, and coiners had liquid metal poured down their throats. A noble who killed a moujik was fined or sometimes whipped; but he might kill as many slaves as he pleased, because they were his property.

The Russian infantry, so famous under the early Norsemen, had given way to cavalry, in imitation of the Tartars. The Imperial Guard was composed of 8,000 young nobles. The "men-at-arms" were mounted, but received no pay beyond the revenue of their lands, which they held in return for their military service. The army numbered about 80,000, and, with a levy among the peasants, could be brought up to 300,000. There was, besides, the irregular cavalry of the Don Cossacks, and of the Tartars. Such infantry as there was, consisted of peasants from the crown lands, churches, and convents; the national guard, and foreign soldiers or officers.

R. Van Bergen

XV

FEODOR, THE LAST OF RURIK'S DESCENDANTS

Ivan the Terrible left two sons, Feodor, the son of Anastasia Romanof, and Dmitri, a child, the son of his seventh wife. Feodor was neither a strong-minded nor a very able man. He was married to Irene Godounof, and, following the usual custom, his wife's relations held the principal offices of the government. Gradually the czar's authority passed into the hands of Prince Boris Godounof, Irene's brother, a very ambitious and unscrupulous man. Wizards had foretold that Boris would be czar, but that his reign would last only seven years, and he did all he could to aid his destiny.

He first caused Feodor's half-brother, Dmitri, to be sent with his mother and her relations to Ouglitch, where they would be out of the way. He also caused the Metropolitan to be dismissed, and had a friend appointed in his place. He aroused the higher nobles against him, and then made an effort to make friends with the smaller nobility,—at the expense of the poor peasants. According to law, these people were free; that is, when the contract with a landowner expired, they could move where they pleased, and the large owners could offer better terms than those who held small estates. But without labor, the land was worthless and Russia, at the time, was so sparsely populated, that every hand counted. The object of the government was not to open up new lands, so as to create prosperity, but to provide for its current wants by seeing that the taxes were paid, and that the army was kept up to its standard. How could the men-at-arms, that is the small nobility, defray their own expenses while serving, if their revenues failed from lack of labor? Boris Godounof, therefore, made a law forbidding peasants to go from one estate to another. They were tied to the ground, and this was the first step to make serfs of them. The peasants did object; they had been accustomed to change service on St. George's day, and that day remained for many years one of deep sorrow. There was no rebellion, but a great many fled, and joined the Cossacks. After some years the law was changed so that peasants were permitted to change from one *small* estate to another.

Another change under Feodor's reign was the appointment of a Patriarch as the head of the Greek Church under the czar. He was placed above the several Metropolitans, and thus the Church secured more unity.

Feodor had no heirs, and his health was bad. It was, therefore, to young Dmitri at Ouglitch that the great nobles looked for relief from Godounof's tyranny. In 1591, this man sent hired assassins to Ouglitch and the youngest son of Ivan was murdered. Some of the hirelings were arrested by the people, and put to death. There was not even a doubt as to the facts. But Godounof ordered an investigation by his own friends; they declared that the young heir had committed suicide in a fit of insanity, and that the people of Ouglitch had put innocent men to death. The assassination of Dmitri's relatives, and the depopulation of Ouglitch made further inquiry impossible.

Stephen Batory who had worsted Ivan the Terrible, died in 1586, and the throne of Poland was once again vacant.

Godounof tried hard to have Feodor elected, but the Poles feared that the czar might attach their kingdom to Moscow like a sleeve to a coat. Besides, the Roman Catholic electors did not like the thought of having a king belonging to the Greek Church; last of all, money counted in these elections, and Godounof was a very saving man. The result was that the Prince of Sweden was elected, and that war with Sweden broke out.

The Poles, fearing lest Sweden should grow too powerful, held aloof; as a consequence, Russia gained back the towns which had been lost under Ivan the Terrible. Godounof made an effort to bring about a war between Poland and Sweden, but he only succeeded in arousing the suspicion and dislike of both countries.

Feodor died in 1598; with him the house of Rurik, the old Norse Viking, ceased to exist.

By trickery and knavery, Boris Godounof was elected czar by the *douma* or council of nobles, a body presided over by his friend the Patriarch, and containing many of his partisans. The great nobles, many of whom traced their descent to Rurik, objected to a czar, whom they considered and called an upstart. But Boris displayed cruelty as well as severity. Feodor, the eldest of the noble family of the Romanofs, was forced to become a monk and his wife a nun. He took the name of Philarete, and she that of Marfa.

Godounof did reign seven years, according to the wizard's prediction, but it was a stormy time for Russia. A young adventurer named Gregory Otrepief, pretended that he was the murdered Dmitri, and secured a large following. The troops sent against him "had no hands to fight but only feet to fly." At Godounof's death, in 1605, he confided his son and heir to a favorite named Basmanof, who turned traitor, joined the false Dmitri, and caused Godounof's widow and son to be murdered. Otrepief, who lacked neither courage nor ability, was made czar, but he reigned little over a month, when he, too, was murdered by a band of nobles under the leadership of Chouiski. This man seized the throne in 1606. The people in the country, owing to its vast extent and the poor roads, heard of Otrepief's coronation, his death, and the succession of Chouiski almost at the same time, and anarchy followed. At the same time Russia was involved in a war with Poland, at the time when a second false Dmitri made his appearance. The Cossacks and a host of Polish adventurers joined him, and he laid siege to the immensely wealthy Troitsa monastery, where the monks defended themselves for sixteen months, and he was forced to withdraw. Affairs came to such a pass that the people of Moscow "humbly requested the czar to abdicate, because he was not successful, and also because he was to blame for the shedding of Christian blood." Chouiski was forced to yield, and soon after entered a monastery as a monk.

Two candidates appeared for the vacant throne; the second false Dmitri and Vladislas, the second son of Sigismund, King of Poland. The douma, not fancying the idea that an impostor should rule over them, invited the hetman of a Polish army to Moscow, to discuss the other candidate. This hetman promised in name of the prince to maintain the Greek Church and the privileges of the three orders, nobles, priests, and people, and that the law-making power should be shared by the czar and the douma; that no one should be executed without a trial, or deprived of his dignity without good reason; and finally, that Russians might go abroad to be educated if they so desired. Vladislas was then elected czar on condition that he should enter the Greek Church, and two envoys, one of them Philarete Romanof who had risen to the rank of Metropolitan, left for the Polish camp at Smolensk to complete the necessary arrangements. The douma invited the hetman to occupy the kremlin with his shoulders. He did so, taking the late Czar Chouiski and his two brothers as hostages.

At Smolensk a difficulty occurred: the King of Poland wanted the Russian throne for himself. He also asked the envoys to cede Smolensk to Poland; they refused, and in turn asked that Vladislas should leave at once for Moscow. The king refused his consent, and began to use money. He found many Russian traitors willing to accept it, but the envoys remained firm.

Soon after this, the second false Dmitri died, and the people began to show an interest in the dispute with Sigismund. Leading men at Moscow and Smolensk wrote to the provinces, begging their friends not to recognize the King of Poland as czar. Men-at-arms gathered, and when an army of them drew near Moscow, the Poles fortified the Kremlin. At this time a quarrel arose between the Polish troops and the people, and some 7,000 persons were killed. The Russians made a stand in the suburbs, when the Poles set fire to the city, and the greater part of Moscow was burned.

Sigismund ordered the arrest of the two envoys who were taken to Marienburg in Prussia under escort. Smolensk fell soon after into his hands, and the king returned to Warsaw which he entered in triumph with the last Czar Chouiski a prisoner in his train. By this time the Russians were aroused; 100,000 men-at-arms gathered at Moscow and besieged the Poles in the Kremlin. Meanwhile Sweden had declared war, giving as reason the election of Vladislas, and had captured the ports on the Baltic. The monks of Troitsa, whose heroic defense against the second false Dmitri had made the convent famous, sent letters to all the Russian cities bidding them fight for their country and religion. When this letter was read in public at Nishni Novgorod, a butcher, Kouzma

Minine spoke up: "If we wish to save the Muscovite Empire," he said, "we must spare neither our lands nor our goods; let us sell our houses and put our wives and children out to service; let us seek a man who will fight for the national faith, and march under his banner." He set the example by giving one-third of all he possessed, and others followed. Those who refused to contribute were compelled to do so. Minine was elected treasurer; he accepted on condition that his orders should be obeyed without delay. Believing that the leadership should be given to a noble, Minine went to Prince Pojarski who lived in the neighborhood. Pojarski accepted the command, and ordered three days of fasting and prayer. The streltsi were equipped as well as the men-at-arms; but the services of Cossacks and foreign mercenaries were refused.

An army was collected and marched toward Moscow, with bishops and monks carrying holy eikons at the head; at Iaroslaf they were reenforced by other troops. They laid siege to the Kremlin; an attempt to relieve the fortress by the Poles was defeated. At last the garrison was forced to surrender. Among the Russian prisoners who regained their liberty was a fifteen-year-old boy, Michael Romanof, the son of Philarete and Marfa.

Sigismund was on the way to reenforce the garrison, but hearing of its surrender, he fell back. An assembly was convoked to elect a czar. It was composed of delegates of the clergy, the nobles, the men-at-arms, the merchants, towns, and districts. There was much bickering, but all were agreed that no alien should be presented. When the name of Michael Romanof was called, it was received with enthusiasm, and he was declared elected. (1613.) The delegates remembered the relation between his family and Ivan the Terrible, and the services rendered by his father, the Metropolitan Philarete. There is a story that the King of Poland, when he heard of

Michael's election, tried to kidnap him at Kostroma, and that a peasant guide led the party astray on a dark night. When the Poles discovered it, he was struck dead. This is the subject of a famous opera "A Life for the Czar."

Russia's efforts to resume intercourse with Europe, which during the Tartar yoke had been suspended, were continued under Godounof. He sent an ambassador to Queen Elizabeth with a letter, in which he says:—"I have learned that the Queen had furnished help to the Turks against the Emperor of Germany. We are astonished at it, as to act thus is not proper for Christian sovereigns; and you, our well-beloved sister, you ought not in the future to enter into relationships of friendship with Mussulman princes, nor to help them in any way, whether with men or money; but on the contrary should desire and insist that all the great Christian potentates should have a good understanding, union, and strong friendship, and unite against the Mussulmans, till the hand of the Christian rise and that of the Mussulman is abased." Judging from Elizabeth's character, it is likely that she shrugged her shoulders as she read this sermon. During the period of Russia's internal troubles, and owing to the vacancy of the throne, the relations with Europe were again suspended.

XVI

MICHAEL FEODOROVITCH OR MICHAEL, THE SON OF THEODORE, THE FIRST ROMANOF

Fifteen years of anarchy left Russia in disorder. The boyards had done as they pleased since there was no one to control them. The peasants who asked for nothing but a simple existence, had seen their crops trampled under foot, and their homes laid in ruins. It needed a strong hand to restore order; more than could be expected from a fifteen-year-old boy, who had neither the iron will of Ivan the Terrible, nor the advantage of having grown up with the conviction that he was the Master. Besides, although his election had been regular, the Don Cossacks and others refused to recognize him as the czar. On the other hand, the patriots stood by him. But the conditions were such that a foreigner in Moscow wrote at the time: "Oh that God would open the eyes of the czar as He opened those of Ivan, otherwise Muscovy is lost!"

There was no money in the treasury, and the men-at-arms demanded pay because they received no revenues from their ruined estates. The czar and the clergy wrote to the Russian towns begging them for money and for troops to help the government, and a generous response was made. The people of the provinces, anxious to see law and order restored, rose in favor of the czar, and Astrakhan sent a rebel chief to prison. He was shortly afterwards tried and executed.

While the people were thus aiding the government, no time was lost in dealing with the foreign enemy. In 1614, Michael sent envoys to Holland to request help in men and money. The Dutch gave a small sum, regretting that they could do no more as they had just ended a war that had lasted forty-one years (1568-1609); they promised that they would persuade Sweden to come to an understanding with Russia. Another embassy went to James I of England, who was told that the Poles had murdered British merchants and plundered their warehouses. This was a falsehood, because the envoys knew that the outrage had been committed by Cossacks and a Russian mob, but they hoped that the king would not know it. James did not, and advanced 20,000 rubles. After this British merchants demanded concessions and privileges in Russia, but as they asked too much, they received nothing. Sweden, urged by England and Holland, concluded with Russia the Peace of Stolbovo in 1617. Sweden received an indemnity of 20,000 rubles, and surrendered Novgorod and other towns.

The war with Poland was then continued more vigorously, and in 1618 a truce of fourteen years and six months was arranged. It was understood that this was temporary, because the King of Poland still claimed the throne of Russia, and refused to recognize Michael. But the prisoners were released and Philarete, the czar's father, returned to Moscow, where his presence was soon felt by the nobles. The most independent were arrested and sent into exile. So long as Philarete assisted his son, there was no disorder.

In 1618, the great struggle between Protestant and Roman Catholic Europe began and Sweden, which was to take such a glorious part in it, sought Russia's aid. Gustavus wrote to Michael telling him that if the Catholic league should prevail, the Greek Church would be in danger. "When your neighbor's house is on fire," he wrote, "you must bring water and try to extinguish it, to guarantee your own safety. May your Czarian Majesty help your neighbors to protect yourself." Sound as the advice was, Russia had enough to do at home. Sultan Osman of Turkey offered an alliance against Poland, when Michael convoked the Estates. The deputies beat their foreheads, and implored the czar "to hold himself firm for the holy churches of God, for his czarian honor, and for their own country against the enemy. The men-at-arms were ready to fight, and the merchants to give money." The war was postponed when news arrived that the Turks had been defeated.

Sigismund of Poland died in 1632, and his son Vladislas was elected. The following year Philarete died, and the nobles, released from his stern supervision, resumed their former behavior. The war between the two neighbors recommenced, but did not last long. When a new truce was concluded Michael's title as czar was recognized by Vladislas.

It was entirely the fault of the Polish nobles that Poland lost Lithuania or White Russia. The only excuse that can be offered, is the spirit of religious persecution which was rampant all over Europe in the seventeenth century. It was the ceaseless effort of the Poles to force the Lithuanians from the Greek into the Roman Church that drove them into the arms of Russia; but it was not until after the death of Michael, in 1645, that the consequences of this short-sighted policy were to show.

Michael was succeeded by his son, who ascended the throne as Alexis Michaelovitch. He was better educated than his father had been and resembled him in good nature. He had been taught by a tutor named Morozof, who during thirty years exerted a great influence over his pupil. When Alexis married into the Miloslavski family, its members secured the most influential positions, according to well-established custom. Morozof did not oppose them; instead he courted and married the czarina's sister, and thus became the czar's brother-in-law.

The wars in which Russia was engaged and the necessity of maintaining a large and well-equipped army, together with the increasing expenses of the Court, and above all, the dishonest practices of the officials rendered the burden of taxation so unbearable, that several revolts broke out. In 1648, the people of Moscow rose and demanded the surrender of a judge and another officer, both of whom were notoriously corrupt; the two men were promptly murdered. Then the popular fury turned upon Morozof, who would have suffered the same fate, had not the czar helped him to escape. The government was helpless. In some places, such as Pskof, Novgorod, and elsewhere, the streltsi joined the people, and Russia was for some time at the mercy of an enemy.

It was fortunate for Russia that just at that time, Poland had serious trouble at home. A Cossack, owner of a large estate, educated and brave, was ill-treated and imprisoned by a Polish landowner; and his little son was publicly whipped. He went to Warsaw and laid his complaint before the king. Vladislas told him plainly that the nobles were beyond his control; then, pointing to his sword, he asked if the Cossack could not help himself. The Cossack took the hint, went home, and when the Polish landowners tried to arrest him, he fled to the Khan of the Crimea, interested him in his cause and returned at the head of a Mussulman army. Lithuania rose in rebellion against Poland; the governors and nobles, and especially the priests of the Catholic Church, were hunted down, and those of the Greek Church took revenge for recent injuries and insults.

Vladislas died, and the Diet elected his brother John Casimir. He tried to reduce the very serious rebellion by promises, but there was too deep a hatred between the two churches. Meanwhile order had been restored in Russia, when the people of Lithuania wrote to the czar begging him to take them under his protection. Alexis convoked the Estates, told them that he had been insulted by Poland, and that the Poles were persecuting the members of the Greek Church. They declared in favor of war, and a boyard was sent to Kief to receive the oath of allegiance. The people were willing provided their liberties would be respected. This the czar promised. He declared that the privileges of the Assembly and of the towns would be maintained, that only natives would be employed in the administration and in taxation.

Poland was now sorely pressed. Charles X of Sweden invaded the kingdom and took two of its capitals. The Cossack and Lithuanians entered it from the south, and the Czar Alexis at the head of his own army attacked it on the east. He maintained strict discipline so that the Polish Governors said, "Moscow makes war in quite a new way, and conquers the people by the clemency and good-nature of the czar." The towns of White Russia opened their gates to his army, and Smolensk surrendered after a five weeks' siege. The Swedes captured Warsaw, the last capital of the misruled kingdom.

It was the jealousy of its enemies that saved Poland this time. Alexis entered into a truce and attacked Sweden. This war was carried on from 1656 until 1661, and ended by the peace of Cardis whereby neither country gained any advantage. The Poles, seeing the danger they had incurred, rallied, and once again war broke out with Russia. It was carried on with various success until both countries were exhausted. In 1661, a thirteen years' truce was concluded, whereby Russia restored Lithuania, but kept Little Russia on the left bank of the Dnieper, together with Kief and Smolensk.

In 1668, a revolt was organized by the Metropolitan of Kief, who preferred the jurisdiction of the Patriarch of Constantinople to that of Moscow. As a result, Little Russia was subject to all the horrors of war, but the Russian power prevailed in the end. Then the Cossacks of the Don broke out, and until 1671 the territory between that river and the Volga suffered terribly.

Alexis' reign was remarkable for the introduction of so-called "reforms" in the Church, which were confined wholly to ceremonies and externals. The czar supported the "reformer" Nicon, and those who did not agree with him were called *religious madmen* and suffered persecution. The monasteries near Archangel rebelled and troops were sent against them; but it was eight months before the sturdy monks capitulated.

Alexis continued his father's efforts to reestablish intercourse with Western Europe. But the West was only recovering from the terrible Thirty Years' War, so that little interest was shown.

Alexis had married twice. From the first marriage he had two sons Feodor and Ivan, and six daughters; by his second wife he had one son, Peter, and two daughters. When he died, in 1676, he was succeeded by his eldest son Feodor.

Feodor Alexievitch, the third czar of the Romanof family, reigned only six years, from 1676 to 1682. It was under his reign that a truce for twenty years with Turkey, restored peace to White Russia.

Hitherto Russia had suffered from the rivalry resulting from disputes caused by precedence of birth; generals had lost battles, because they refused to serve under men whom they looked upon as inferiors. At an assembly of the higher clergy, it was resolved to burn the Book of Rank, and the czar made a law that any one disputing about his rank, should lose it as well as his property.

To protect the Greek Church from dividing into sects, an academy was founded at Moscow where the Slav, Latin, and Greek languages were taught.

XVII

EARLY YEARS OF PETER THE GREAT
(PETER ALEXIEVITCH)

Feodor died childless, and should have been succeeded by his little brother Ivan, but the child was of unsound mind. The other son of Alexis, Peter, was the child of his last wife, and nine years old at the time. The question about the succession was discussed in the Council, and decided in Peter's favor, and his mother Natalia became Regent. Among Peter's half sisters was one, Sophia, twenty-five years old, who did not propose to submit to this decision. She took part in Feodor's funeral, in defiance of the law which forbade women to appear in public, and after it schemed and plotted to form a party in her favor. A rumor was spread that the czarina's brother had seized the throne and that Ivan had been murdered. The people of Moscow rose, and the streltsi marched to the kremlin where the appearance of Natalia with the two children made the mob hesitate. Unfortunately Prince Dolgorouki addressed the men in violent language; they seized him on their pikes and killed him. They then stabbed the czarina's foster father, Matveef, in her presence, and sacked the palace, murdering many of its inmates. One of Natalia's brothers was thrown out of a window and caught on the points of the lances of the streltsi who were waiting below. Natalia's father and brother were taken from her;

Cyril, the father, was sent to a monastery and her brother Ivan was tortured and cut to pieces, although the czarina went on her knees begging for his life. The streltsi acted under authority from Sophia when they committed these outrages. After this rioting had continued seven days, the streltsi sent their commandant Khovanski to the douma, to demand that there should be two czars, Ivan, with Peter as his assistant. The douma did not fancy the idea,—but there were the streltsi with their pikes, and they carried the day.

From this time it was Sophia who was the real czar. She reigned in name of the two half-brothers, and showed herself in public, insisting upon being present on every occasion. The Russians as a rule are not fond of new fashions; they did not like this, and objected so strongly that Sophia was forced to give way. Thereafter the two young czars sat in public on the throne, but it was constructed in such a manner that Sophia could hear and see without being visible.

She shocked every Russian by her manners until the streltsi began to speak of her as "the scandalous person." They hated her when she persecuted the *raskolnik* or Old Believers, that is, the men who objected to the reforms of Nicon. At last she thought that it was not safe for her to remain at Moscow; she fled to the strong convent at Troitsa, taking with her the czarina and the two little tsars, and there summoned the men-at-arms whom she could trust. Khovanski, the commandant of the streltsi, was summoned before her; he was arrested on the way, and put to death with his son. The streltsi were considering another revolt, when they were seized with a panic; instead of marching upon Troitsa, they went there to beg her pardon. Sophia forgave them, but their leaders were executed.

Sophia trusted the government to two favorites, Prince Galitsyne who was at the head of Foreign Affairs, and

Chaklovity whom she made commandant of the streltsi. Galitsyne tried hard to form an alliance among the Christian powers against the Turks and Tartars. His scheme failed because Louis XIV of France kept the whole of Western Europe in turmoil by his constant wars with the House of Austria, and the Christian princes had to look after their own interests. He was more fortunate in Poland where John Sobieski was king. A treaty of "perpetual" peace was concluded between Russia and Poland at Androussovo, in 1686, and an alliance was entered into against the Turks.

In 1687, an army of 100,000 Russians and 50,000 Cossacks marched against the Crimea. The Tartars had burned the steppes, and the Russians suffered such severe hardships that they were forced to retreat. The hetman of the Cossacks was accused of treachery, and deported to Siberia, when Mazeppa, who had been his secretary, was appointed hetman. In the spring of 1689, the Russians under Galitsyne and the Cossacks under Mazeppa started again for the Crimea, but they had no better success than before.

Peter, who was born in 1673, was then sixteen years old, but being tall and strongly built, he looked much older. He was bright and anxious to learn, and at an early age had shown that he possessed a will of his own. He had read much, but his tutor, a man named Zorof, had allowed him to have his own way, and when the boy grew up to be a man, he made that tutor "the arch-priest of fools." When the boy was tired, Zorof would allow him to put his work aside, and would read to him about the great deeds of his father Alexis, and of those of Ivan the Terrible, their campaigns, battles, and sieges; how they endured privations better than the common soldiers, and how they added other territory to Russia. He also learned Latin, German, and Dutch. He afterwards complained that his education was neglected, because he was allowed to do as he pleased. He chose his own companions, and as he did not like to be confined within the palace grounds, he roamed in the streets and often became acquainted with men whom he would not have met in the palace, Russians, Dutch, Swiss, English, and Germans. His usual attendants were Boris Galitsyne and other young nobles with whom he played at soldier. He pressed the palace servants into the ranks and had them drilled in European tactics. Peter took lessons in geometry and fortification; he constructed small forts which were besieged and defended by the young players. Sometimes the game became earnest; blows were given and received, when Peter took his share without a murmur, even when he was wounded as sometimes happened.

At first Peter did not like the water; no Russian does; but he mastered his dislike. Once, when he saw a stranded English boat, he sent for a boatbuilder to make him a sailboat and to teach him how to manage it. He took a great fancy to sailing, and often took his boat on the Yaousa, and afterwards on Lake Pereiaslaf, to the terror of his mother. Thus Peter grew up, healthy in body and strong of mind, until his ambitious half-sister Sophia began to think what would become of her when the boy should be czar. She had styled herself Autocrat of all the Russias and did not like the idea of surrendering the title. For some time she was appeased when her courtiers told her that the boy cared for nothing except to amuse himself.

When he was sixteen years old, Peter asserted himself. Sophia had ordered a triumphal entry for Prince Galitsyne and the army of the Crimea, when Peter forbade her to leave the palace. She paid no attention to his orders, but headed the procession of the returned army. Peter saw that this meant war to the knife, and left for Preobajenskoe.

As soon as she heard of this, Sophia determined to seize the

R. Van Bergen

throne. She intended to attack the palace, kill Peter's friends and arrest his mother, and after that to deal with the young czar as circumstances demanded. She sent for the commandant of the streltsi who agreed to sound the men. He told them that Sophia's life was in danger, and that she had fled to a convent. The latter part of the story was true, as she had in fact retreated to such a place, from which she sent letters to the streltsi to come to her rescue. The commandant failed to secure more than 500 men; the other streltsi told him that there should be an investigation.

Two of the streltsi went to Peter and reported to him what was going on, whereupon he moved to the famous Troitsa monastery. The Patriarch, foreign officers serving in the army, his playmates, and even a regiment of streltsi came to him to offer their services. Peter issued orders for the arrest of Sophia's favorite, the commandant of the militia. She begged the Patriarch to interfere but met with a refusal. The commandant under torture confessed the plot, and was beheaded. Sophia's other friends were arrested; some were executed while others were sent to prison; she herself was confined in the convent where she had found a retreat. Peter was now the czar, although he conducted the government in his own name and in that of his weak-minded brother Ivan.

If Sophia had shocked the Russians by leaving the seclusion of the women's apartments, Peter's acts were likely to astonish them still more and to give offense. Rowing in a boat, instead of sitting in it surrounded by his grandees; working like a carpenter, instead of merely giving his orders through a courtier, and fighting with foreigners and grooms, were acts so unlike to what a czar should do, that Peter made a host of enemies. Little did he care! No sooner was he free to do as he pleased, than he rushed off to Archangel, the only port Russia could call her own, and there he saw salt water for the first time. He mingled freely with captains of the foreign merchant vessels and went out in their boats. On one occasion, he was out in a storm and came near being drowned; but this did not prevent "Skipper Peter Alexievitch," from putting out to sea again. Once he piloted three Dutch vessels. The young czar gave orders to construct a dockyard and to have boats built.

Peter longed for ports on an open sea, a sea that would not freeze in winter. There were three which Russia might reasonably hope to own some day, the Baltic, the Black, and the Caspian Sea. The Baltic belonged to Sweden, and Peter feared difficulties in that direction; but the Black Sea belonged to the Turks, and Peter quite understood that a war with the infidels would be popular in Russia. He wished to visit Western Europe; to see for himself the wonders of which he had heard foreigners speak; but he made up his mind not to go until he could appear as a victorious general.

Thus Peter made preparations for war with the Khan of the Crimea. He did not command his army; what he wanted, was to learn, and therefore he went as the gunner Peter Alexievitch. That did not prevent him from keeping a sharp eye on his generals. Chief-engineer Jansen received a sound whipping from him and deserted to the enemy. For this and other causes he was compelled to raise the siege of Azof and to fall back to Russia. His mother died in 1694. He returned to Russia in 1695, and notwithstanding his defeat, he ordered a triumphal entry into Moscow; but he felt very sore. The following year, 1696, his half-brother Ivan died, and Peter was the sole Autocrat of all the Russias.

XVIII

PETER THE GREAT AND HIS REIGN

Far from being discouraged by his defeat, Peter was more than ever resolved to have a port on the Black Sea. He introduced reforms in the army, and while doing this, he ordered a fleet of boats to be built on the Don, and set 26,000 men to work on them. He also sent to Holland and other parts of Europe for officers and gunners, and superintended everything. It was at this time that he wrote to Moscow that, "following the command God gave Adam, he was earning his bread by the sweat of his brow." When he was ready, the army and the boats went down the Don; Azof was blockaded by sea and by land, and forced to capitulate. When the news arrived at Moscow, there was general rejoicing, and even at Warsaw in Poland the people cheered for the czar. The army returned to Moscow under triumphal arches, the generals seated in magnificent sledges. A young officer, Peter Alexievitch, recently promoted to captain, was marching in the ranks.

Peter wished to make of Azof a Russian town in the shortest time possible. He secured from the douma an order by which three thousand families were moved to that port, and streltsi were dispatched to garrison it. The czar wanted a naval force, and moved by his energy, the Patriarch, the prelates, and the monasteries offered to give one ship for every 5,000 serfs owned by them. This example was followed by nobles, officials, and merchants, and once more Peter sent to the west for competent men to help build them. At the same time fifty young nobles were dispatched to Venice to learn shipbuilding.

When he was seventeen years old, Peter had married Eudoxia Lapoukine, whose relatives abhorred all that was new; Peter's wife shared their sentiments, so that his home life was far from happy. He had a son by her, named Alexis; after the fall of Azof, Peter secured a divorce, an act unheard of in Russia, where she remained czarina in the eyes of the people. Busy as he was, Peter left his son and heir in charge of his divorced wife, while he was making preparations for the long expected visit to the west of Europe.

He determined that an embassy should be sent, and that it should be worthy of Russia. Accordingly he appointed the Swiss Lafort and two Russian generals "the great Ambassadors of the Czar." Among their retinue composed of two hundred and seventy persons, was a young man Peter Mikhailof, better known as Peter Alexievitch. When the embassy came to Riga, that young man was insulted by the governor. Peter said nothing, but made a note of it for future use. At Koenigsberg, "Mr. Peter Mikhailof" was appointed master of artillery by the Prussian Colonel Sternfeld. The progress of the embassy was too slow for Peter who had an object in view. He went ahead to Holland where he hired a room from a blacksmith at Zaandam, bought a workman's suit, and went to work in a dockyard. He often visited Amsterdam where his good nature and passion to learn gained him the good-will of the people. Peter then crossed over to London where he spent three months. Competent men of every profession and trade were engaged by him everywhere. Returning to Holland, his ship was caught in a violent gale, which frightened even the sailors. Peter kept cool, and, smiling, asked them if they "had ever heard of a Czar of Russia who was drowned in the North Sea?"

Peter did not forget Russia's political interests. He talked with William of Orange, the great opponent of Louis XIV, and with other influential men, but he did not visit the court of France. After satisfying his curiosity, he went to Vienna where he intended to study strategy; but his stay was cut short by bad news from home.

Peter had met with a sullen, obstinate opposition in Russia. It was led by the priests who said, and perhaps believed, that Peter was the anti-Christ. It was a cause for complaint that Peter often wore clothes of a German fashion; was the Russian costume not good enough for him? Again, why did he not devote his time to war, as the other czars had done? He had made a bargain with British merchants to import tobacco into Russia; what did the Russians want with this "sacrilegious smell?" But the climax was that a *Czar of the Russias* should leave Holy Russia to go among heretics and heathens. Geography was not studied in the czar's empire, and all nations on earth were thought to belong to either of the two classes.

The trouble began among the streltsi who had been sent to Azof. These citizen soldiers looked upon their destination at the other end of the empire as an exile,—which it may have been. Two hundred deserted and made their way back to Moscow and their families; they were promptly hunted down. When they returned to their regiments, they brought with them a secret proclamation from Sophia. "You suffer," she declared, "but it will grow worse still. March on Moscow! What are you waiting for? There is no news of the czar!" There was a rumor that Peter was dead and that his son Alexis had been murdered by the boyards. Four regiments revolted and left the ranks. Generals Gordon and Schein went after them with the regular troops, and after overtaking the mutineers, tried to bring them to reason. In reply they stated their grievances and persisted in their determination not to return to duty. The government troops then fired and scattered the streltsi. A number of them were arrested, tortured, and executed.

At this time Peter returned, furious at what had happened. He was determined to strike at the head of the opposition, the Russians who openly denounced innovations. He ordered that the face must be shaved. This was hitting every adult Russian in a tender spot, because the shaving of the face was considered in the light of a blasphemy. He began to enforce his orders at his court, sometimes acting as a barber himself, when he was none too gentle. A number of gibbets erected on the Red Square, reminded the bearded noble that the choice lay between losing the beard or the head. The Patriarch appealed to Peter, a holy eikon of the Virgin in his hand. "Why did you bring out the holy eikon?" asked the czar. "Withdraw and restore it to its place. Know that I venerate God and His mother as much as you do, but know also that it is my duty to protect the people and to punish the rebels."

The gibbets did not stand as an idle threat. The Austrian Minister Korb was a witness of the executions, which he describes thus: "Five rebel heads had been sent into the dust by blows from an ax wielded by the noblest hand in Russia." Thus Peter did not hesitate to be his own executioner. It was like him to do his own work, regardless of what the people might think. A thousand men were sent to a gory grave, by the highest officers of the court; the executions lasted a week. The funeral of the executed was forbidden. Bodies were seen dangling from the walls of the kremlin for five months, and for the same length of time, the corpses of some of the streltsi hung from the bars of Sophia's prison, clutching the secret proclamation. Peter's divorced wife had joined Sophia's party; the two ladies had their head shaved and were confined in convents. The streltsi were dissolved and replaced by regular troops.

Peter then turned upon the Cossacks of the Don, who had shown greater independence than pleased him. Prince Dolgorouki to whom the task was confided of bringing them to order, wrote to the czar after he had destroyed the Cossack camp: "The chief rebels and traitors have been hung; of the others, one out of every ten; and all these dead malefactors have been laid on rafts, and turned into the river, to strike terror into the hearts of the Don people and to cause them to repent."

Mazeppa, as we have seen, was at this time hetman of the Cossacks of Little Russia. In his youth he had been a page of John Casimir, king of Poland; it was then that he had that terrible adventure which is connected indelibly with his name. After he was cut loose from the back of the unbroken horse that had carried him in the steppes, he entered among the Cossacks, and rose from the ranks by betraying every chief who helped him. Although it was Sophia who made him hetman, he was among the first to declare for Peter. His enemies, of whom he had many, accused him before the czar, but Peter admired him, and delivered his accusers up to him; they did not live long after Mazeppa had them in his power.

It was Mazeppa's scheme to establish an independent kingdom, he had the support of the Cossacks who did not care to work but preferred to be supported by the people. The industrious classes longed to get rid of this burden, and looked toward the czar to set them free. The tribute which Little Russia paid to Moscow was quite heavy, and when it was rumored that Peter was going to war with Sweden, Mazeppa thought this was an opportunity to carry out his scheme. He entered into negotiations with Stanislas Lecszinski whom Swedish influence had placed upon the throne of Poland. Peter was informed of this in detail, but he did not credit it, beheaded one of his informants, and the others, were tortured and sent to Siberia.

The war broke out, Charles XII, the romantic king of Sweden arrived in the neighborhood of Little Russia, and Peter called on Mazeppa to join the Russian army with his Cossacks. He pretended to be dying, but when the two hostile armies were drawing close, he crossed the Desna with his most trusted Cossacks to join the Swedes. Peter's eyes were opened; he gave orders to his general Menzikoff to take and sack Mazeppa's capital. This was done and Mazeppa's friends, who had remained behind, were executed. Mazeppa himself reached the Swedish camp. He was compelled to seek safety in Turkey, where he died miserably at Bender. His territory was annexed to Russia, the Cossacks lost all their privileges, and 1,200 of them were set to work on the Ladoga canal.

It was in 1700 that Peter, after concluding an alliance with Poland, determined to declare war against Sweden where young Charles XII had recently succeeded to the throne. Attacked at the same time by Russia, Poland, and Denmark, this young hero invaded the last-named country and compelled its king to conclude peace. After relieving Riga, Charles marched into Russia at the head of 8,500 men, and on the 30th of November defeated a Russian army of 63,000 men. This victory proved a misfortune, because it inspired the King of Sweden with contempt for Russian soldiers and made him careless, whereas Peter worked cheerfully and hard to profit from the lesson. While Charles was absent in Poland, his army was twice defeated.

R. Van Bergen

Each of the two antagonists was worthy of the other's steel. Both were brave, but Charles was impetuous, whereas Peter acted upon cool judgment. The war continued until 1709 when Charles found himself in Little Russia, far away from supplies and reinforcements, in a Russian winter which happened to be exceptionally severe. In the spring he laid siege to Pultowa. The czar arrived on the 15th of June with 60,000 men; Charles had 29,000. On July 8, 1709, the battle of Pultowa was fought and Charles was defeated; he narrowly escaped being captured. With Mazeppa and the Pole Poniatowski, he made his way across the Turkish frontier, and remained until 1713, in the territory of the Sultan, whom he finally induced to declare war against Peter. This victory gave Peter the longed-for port on the Baltic, since Sweden was no longer in a condition to stop him.

What induced Sultan Ahmed III to risk war with Russia, was the hope of regaining Azof. Peter, on the other hand, hoped for an opportunity to capture Constantinople, the Czargrad of former times. He knew that he had the sympathy of the many Christians of the Greek Church, who were suffering under the yoke of the Turk. Trusting upon their support, Peter arrived on the bank of the Pruth with 38,000 exhausted soldiers. There he found himself surrounded by 200,000 Turks and Tartars. Peter gained a slight success, but not of sufficient importance to extricate or relieve him. Fearing an overwhelming calamity, Peter was prepared to make immense sacrifices in return for peace, and even to surrender Azof and the territory taken from Sweden, when his second wife Catherine had a happy thought. She collected all the money and jewels in the Russian camp, and sent them as a present to the Grand Vizier in command of the enemy, asking at the same time, what terms he would make. They were found unexpectedly reasonable: the surrender of Azof, the razing of the Russian forts erected on Turkish territory, and that Charles XII should be free to return to Sweden.

Peter accepted eagerly, much as he regretted the loss of Azof and the failure of his schemes.

In 1713, a Russian fleet under Admiral Apraxine, with Peter serving under him as vice-admiral, captured several cities on the Baltic, and a Russian force entered north Germany. An alliance was formed against him and Peter decided to make an attempt at an alliance with France. In 1718, just as peace was being concluded with Charles XII, the King of Sweden, died and war broke out anew, lasting until 1721, when, by the Peace of Nystad, Sweden surrendered to Russia Livonia, Esthonia, and part of Finland. Peter had his way: Russia had open ports.

Peter was greatly pleased, and Russia rejoiced with him. The senate and Holy Synod conferred upon him the titles of "the Great, the Father of his country, and Emperor of all the Russias." In 1722, Peter led an expedition to the Caspian Sea. He captured Baku and five other important towns. He died three years later, in 1725.

XIX

PETER THE GREAT AND HIS TIME

Before judging Peter the Great, the time in which he lived, and the conditions which prevailed should receive careful consideration. Throughout Western Europe, in France, Germany, Spain, and Italy, in parliamentary England and republican Holland, the people, that is the masses, toiled early and late for the privilege of paying the taxes; all immunities were reserved for the favored few composing the aristocracy.

There was no education among the people, with the exception perhaps of Holland, then still a power of the first rank. The principle was that the interests of the individual were unworthy of consideration by the side of those of the State. That was the case in France as well as in Russia. Peter inherited the idea of autocratic power, and his travels in Europe conveyed to him nothing to upset or contradict that idea. He cannot, therefore, be considered in the light of a tyrant. He acted, so far as he could know, within his prerogative, and did his duty as he saw it.

Russia, with a thin and scattered population largely engaged in agriculture, felt no impulse toward progress. The moujik lived as his father had lived. He never came in contact with people of a superior civilization who, by introducing new wants, could make him discontented with his lot. Knowing no desire but to satisfy his physical craving, he bore the extremes of heat and cold with equal fortitude; the soil and his labor provided for his subsistence. A life so sordid must either brutalize man or feed his imagination with the unknown and dreaded forces of nature; superstition, deep and strong, became part of the peasant's existence. It is generations before a traditional and deep-rooted belief can be eradicated.

But Peter the Great gave as little thought to the moujik as did Louis XIV to the peasants of France. His influence was exerted upon the boyards, and among them the opposition was the stronger as they had been imbued with Asiatic ideas under the Tartar yoke. Here the great muscular strength of Peter rendered him great service. He did not hesitate to use a stick upon the highest officials any more than Ivan the Terrible had used his iron-tipped staff. Even Menzikoff was chastized in this manner. Frederick the Great of Prussia did the same afterwards. Nor was this method of punishing without its use. One day when Peter was looking over the accounts of one of his nobles, he proved to him that, whereas the boyard had been robbing the government, he in turn had been robbed by his steward. The czar took the noble by the collar and applied the stick with a muscular arm and great vigor. After he had punished him to his heart's content, he let him go, saying, "Now you had better go find your steward and settle accounts with him."

It was Peter's purpose to make the Russians again into Europeans. He rightly deemed it best to begin with externals, because they are the object lessons of changes. The Russian boyard was attached to the long caftan or tunic adopted from the Tartars, but above all he was devoted to the hair on his face. The beard was doomed by the czar. He could not play barber to all his subjects, but he imposed a heavy tax upon unshaven faces. Owners of beards paid from thirty to one hundred rubles, and moujiks had to pay two pence for theirs every time they entered a city or town.

The reform which had the most lasting influence upon Russia, was the abolition of the landed nobility as a separate class. They would be known as "*tchin*" or gentlemen, and any one who entered the service of the government, regardless of birth, was at once entitled to be classed among the *tchinovnik*. From that time the terms gentleman and officer, became synonymous. Every service, civil, military, naval, or ecclesiastic, was divided into fourteen grades. The lowest grade in the civil service was held by the registrar of a college, the highest by the Chancellor of the Empire; the cornet was at the bottom, the field marshal at the top in the army; and the deacon in a church was fourteen degrees removed from the Patriarch,—but all were *tchin*.

When, in 1700, the Patriarch Adrian died, the dignity was abolished by Peter who did not relish the idea of a rival power in the State. Instead he created the Holy Synod together with the office of Superintendent of the Patriarchal Throne. He gives his reasons in the ukase wherein the change is announced. "The simple people," this document reads, "are not quick to seize the distinction between the spiritual and imperial power; struck with the virtue and the splendor of the supreme pastor of the Church, they imagine that he is a second sovereign, equal and even superior in power to the Autocrat."

The Holy Synod consisted of bishops and a Procurator-general who represented the czar and as such could veto any resolution. This official was often a general. Every bishop had to keep a school in his palace, and the sons of priests who refused to attend were taken as soldiers. Autocrat though he was, Peter dared not confiscate the property of the monasteries, but he forbade any person to enter a convent before his thirtieth year. The monks were ordered to work at some trade, or to teach in the schools and colleges. At this time, the Protestant and Catholic churches of the West tried to make converts, and the *raskols* were hostile to the national church. As a rule Peter did not favor persecution; so long as the church did not interfere with his authority, there was nothing to fear from him; but upon the slightest suspicion his heavy hand was felt. Thus, in 1710, he suddenly ordered the expulsion of the Jesuits. He used to say: "God has given the czar power over the nations, but Christ alone has power over the conscience of man." This did not prevent him from exacting a double tax from the raskols in Moscow, nor from punishing cruelly any Russian converted to one of the western churches.

The great mass of the people suffered severely by Peter's reforms. The peasants as tenants of the large landowners had enjoyed some liberty and were legally free men; they were by him assigned to the soil, which they were not permitted to leave. Thus they, too, passed into serfdom. If the proprietor sold the estate, the rural population went with it. The owners paid a poll-tax for their serfs. These unfortunates could also be sold without the land, but the czar made a law that "If the sale cannot be abolished completely, serfs must be sold by families without separating husbands from wives, parents from children, and no longer like cattle, a thing unheard of in the whole world."

The citizens of towns were divided into three classes; to the first class belonged bankers, manufacturers, rich merchants, physicians, chemists, capitalists, jewelers, workers in metal, and artists; storekeepers and master mechanics were in the second; all other people belonged to the third. Foreigners could engage in business, acquire real estate; but they could not depart from the country without paying to the government one tenth of all they possessed.

Cities and towns were administered by burgomasters elected by the citizens; this board selected its own president or mayor. If an important question arose, representatives of the first two classes were summoned for consultation. All the mayors of Russia were subject to a magistrate selected from the Council of St. Petersburg, and appointed by the czar. This official watched over the interests of commerce and agriculture, settled disputes between citizens and burgomasters, confirmed local elections, authorized executions when a death sentence was pronounced by provincial authorities, and made reports to the tsar.

The *voievodes* or governors of a province directed all the affairs of their jurisdiction and disbursed the revenues as they thought best. "Help yourself first!" was the unwritten law, and it was universally obeyed. Peter divided his empire into forty-three provinces, forming twelve governments each under a viceroy and deputy, who were assisted by a council elected by the nobles.

The courts were crude and mediaeval, but not more so than in the west of Europe. Justice, such as it was, was administered by the General Police Inspector, and in large cities there was a police officer for every ten houses. Servants who failed to keep the house front clean were punished with the knout. Peter created the Bureau of Information, a court of secret police, and thus inaugurated the terrible spy system which still disgraces Russia.

The douma was abolished, and in its stead Peter created a "Directory Senate," which could meet only in presence of the czar. It was originally composed of nine members, but it was afterwards increased and at last embraced the duties of the

Grand Council, the High Finance Committee, and the Supreme Court. A fair idea of the moral and mental condition of Russia's high aristocracy, may be had from a rule made by Peter, forbidding the Senators under severe penalties, while in session "to cry out, to beat each other, or to call one another thieves."

Peter's visits to the west, taught him the value of factories. He gave every possible inducement to foreign capital and skill to come to Russia, and patronized home industry wherever he could, as by purchasing the uniforms for army and navy from recently established mills. Some of his methods appear strange, as, for instance, when he ordered every town in Russia to send a stipulated number of shoemakers to Moscow, to learn their trade. Those who continued to work in the old fashion, were severely punished. The czar would have met with greater success, if he had not been hampered by the cupidity of the officials, who found means to secure the lion's share of the profits.

Peter discarded the old Slavonic alphabet and introduced the one used at present. St. Petersburg had four printing presses, Moscow two, and there were also some at Novgorod, Tchernigof, and other large places. The first newspaper in Russia, the *St. Petersburg Gazette*, was founded by him. He established, in 1724, the Academy of Sciences, in imitation of the institution of that name of Paris.

St. Petersburg was founded in 1703. It was far from a promising site for a new capital, the dreary wastes, dark forests, and marshes where wild ducks and geese found a favorite feeding place. It was exposed to frequent floods, and piles were needed before a building could be erected. But when this autocrat had made up his mind, objections were brushed aside. Peter collected 40,000 men, soldiers, Cossacks, Kalmucks, Tartars and such natives as could be found, and put them to work. At first he provided neither tools nor shelter, and food was often scarce. Thousands of workmen died;—what did he care? Others were compelled to take their place. The fortress of St. Peter and Paul arose first; the czar himself was watching the progress from a little wooden house on the right bank of the Neva. Men of means were forced to build stone houses in the new capital. Swedish prisoners and merchants from Novgorod were invited to move to St. Petersburg, and no excuse was admitted. Goods could be brought only by boat, and no boat was allowed to land unless it carried a certain number of white stones to be used as building material. He erected churches, and ordered that he should be buried in the Church of St. Peter and Paul.

Peter's domestic life, as we have seen, was not happy. After his divorce from his first wife, he married Catherine who, in 1702, had been made prisoner at Marienburg. It is not known where she was born, but she was probably a native of Livonia, and was a servant in the family of Pastor Glueck and engaged to be married to a Swedish dragoon. She became the property of Menzikoff who gave her to the czar. There was a secret marriage which was confirmed by a public ceremony in 1712, in reward for her services at Pultowa. Peter also instituted the Order "For Love and Fidelity," in her honor. A German princess describes her thus:—"The czarina was small and clumsily made, very much tanned, and without grace or air of distinction. You had only to see her to know that she was lowborn. From her usual costume you would have taken her for a German comedian. Her dress had been bought at a secondhand shop; it was very old-fashioned, and covered with silver and dirt. She had a dozen orders, and as many portraits of saints or relics, fastened all down her dress, in such a way that when she walked you would have thought by the jingling that a mule was passing." She could neither read nor write, but she was sharp, had natural wit, and obtained great influence over Peter. They had two sons, Peter and Paul, who died in childhood, and two daughters, Anne and Elizabeth. The former married the Duke of Holstein.

Alexis, the son by his first wife, was Peter's heir. He had grown to be a young man before Peter realized that the result of all his efforts depended upon his successor, and the czar began to pay attention to his son's education when it was too late, when habits had been formed. The czarevitch had imbibed the prejudices of his mother; he was narrow-minded, lazy, weak, and obstinate, and associated with people to whom Old Russia was Holy Russia, who abhorred reforms of every kind. Peter sent him to travel in Germany, but the prince would learn nothing. His father warned him in very plain terms. "Disquiet for the future," he wrote to Alexis, "destroys the joy caused by my present successes. I see that you despise everything that can make you worthy to reign after me. What you call inability, I call rebellion, for you cannot excuse yourself on the ground of the weakness of your mind and the state of your health. We have struggled from obscurity through the toil of war, which has taught other nations to know and respect us, and yet you will not even hear of military exercises. If you do not alter your conduct, know that I shall deprive you of my succession. I have not spared, and I shall not spare, my own life for my country; do you think that I shall spare yours? I would rather have a stranger who is worthy for my heir, than a good-for-nothing member of my own family."

Alexis should have known that his father was in terrible earnest, yet he did not heed the warning. When Peter was traveling in Western Europe, his son fled to Vienna, where he thought that he should be safe. Finding that this was not so, he went to the Tyrol and afterwards to Naples, but his father's agents traced him and one of them, Tolstoi, secured an interview in which he assured the prince of his father's pardon, and finally persuaded him to return to Moscow. As soon as he arrived there, he was arrested. The czar convoked the three Estates before whom he accused the czarevitch. Alexis was forced to sign his resignation of the Crown. When he was being examined, probably under torture, a widespread conspiracy was revealed. Peter learned also that his son had begged the Emperor of Austria for armed intervention, that he had negotiated with Sweden and that he had encouraged a mutiny of the army in Germany. It was shown that his divorced wife and several prelates were in the plot. Peter crushed his enemies. Most of the persons involved suffered a cruel death, and Alexis himself, after being punished with the knout, was sentenced to die. Two days later his death was announced. It appears that on that day, the heir to the throne was brought before a court composed of nine men of the highest rank in Russia and that he was beaten with a knout to secure further confessions, and that he expired under the torture. Those present were sworn to secrecy, and kept the oath.

Peter, therefore, had no male heir. Alexis, however, had left a son Peter by Charlotte of Brunswick whom he married against his will. In 1723 the czar ordered Catherine to be crowned as Empress. He had established the right to select his successor but failed to do so, owing to his sudden death.

The following description of Peter the Great at the age of forty, is given by a Frenchman; "He was a very tall man, well made though rather thin, his face somewhat round, with a broad forehead, beautiful eyebrows, a short nose, thick at the end; his lips were rather thick, his skin was brown and ruddy. He had splendid eyes, large, black, piercing, and well-opened; his expression was dignified and gracious when he liked, but often wild and stern, and his eyes, and indeed his whole face, were distorted by an occasional twitch that was very unpleasant. It lasted only a moment, and gave him a wandering and terrible look, when he was himself again. His air expressed intellect, thoughtfulness, and greatness, and had a certain grace about it. He wore a linen collar, a round wig, brown and unpowdered, which did not reach his shoulders; a brown, tight-fitting coat with gold buttons, a vest, trousers, and stockings, and neither gloves nor cuffs; the star of his order on his coat, and the ribbon underneath it; his coat was often unbuttoned, his hat lay on the table, and was never on his head, even out of doors. In this simplicity, however shabby might be his carriage or scanty his suit, his natural greatness could not be mistaken."

R. Van Bergen

XX

THE SUCCESSORS OF PETER THE GREAT

Peter's strong hand had stifled the opposition to his reforms, but with his death it reappeared. There were, therefore, two parties in Russia: the men who had assisted the dead czar, Menzikoff, Apraxine, Tolstoi, and others, such as the members of the secret Court who had witnessed the violent death of Peter's only son. They dreaded the succession of Peter's grandson, the boy who, although only twelve years old, might order an investigation of his father's death. These men held the power and decided that, since Catherine had been crowned as Empress, it was she who should succeed. Thus the former maid servant, not even a native Russian, became Empress of all the Russias. There were some protests in favor of Peter's grandson, but they were disregarded.

Menzikoff who was the cause of Catherine's rise, fancied himself all-powerful, and there was jealousy among Peter's associates. Menzikoff sent one of them, Tolstoi, to Siberia, but Catherine would not consent to the punishment of the other friends of the late czar. She was honest in carrying out Peter's unfinished projects. He had planned the marriage of his daughter Anne to the Duke of Holstein: the wedding took place; he intended to send an exploring expedition to

Kamtschatka; she engaged the services of a Danish captain, Bering, who discovered the sea and strait named after him. The Academy of Sciences was opened in 1726. She, however, changed the Senate into a Secret High Council, which met under the presidency of the empress.

Catherine died in 1727, and on her deathbed appointed Peter's grandson, then fourteen years old, as her successor. In case of his death, the throne would go to Anne, and next to Elizabeth. During his minority these two daughters assisted by the Duke of Holstein, Menzikoff, and some other high officers, would constitute a Board of Regents.

Menzikoff had taken precautions. He had obtained her consent that the young heir, Peter II, should marry one of his daughters, a young lady two years older than the boy. He showed, in his letters to Peter, that he looked upon him as his son. He also intended his own son to marry the boy's sister Natalia. There was one member of Peter the Great's family who did not approve of Menzikoff's schemes, Elizabeth, the young czar's aunt, then seventeen years old. Not long after Catherine's death, Menzikoff fell ill; he was compelled to keep to his rooms, and in that time Elizabeth roused her nephew's suspicions. Peter left Menzikoff's palace and when Catherine's favorite tried to resume his authority, he was arrested and exiled to his estates. Soon after he was sent to Siberia, where he died two years later, in 1729.

The Dolgorouki family succeeded, but its head committed the same mistakes, besides showing a tendency to undo the work of Peter the Great. The young czar was growing weary of the Dolgorouki when, in January 1730, he caught cold and died after a brief illness.

It was during his short reign that Prussia, Austria, and Russia, first seriously discussed the partition of Poland. A

R. Van Bergen

treaty was signed between Prussia and Russia whereby the two powers agreed to select and support a candidate for the throne of that kingdom which was to illustrate the truth that "a kingdom divided against itself cannot exist."

Peter's death left Russia without a male heir. There were, as we have seen, two daughters from his marriage with Catherine. Anne, who had married the Duke of Holstein, had died in 1728, leaving a son also named Peter. Elizabeth, the other daughter, was in St. Petersburg, quietly engaged in establishing a party of her own. There were, besides, two other parties having claims upon the throne. Ivan, the weak-minded half-brother of Peter the Great, had been married and had left two daughters, Anne, Duchess of Courland, and Catherine, Duchess of Mecklenburg.

The decision rested with the Secret High Council. Dolgorouki's claim, that Peter II had made a secret will leaving the throne to his bride, was laughed to scorn. The members of the High Council saw an opportunity to secure most of the autocratic power for themselves, and resolved to offer the throne to Anne of Courland, provided that she subscribed to the following conditions: That the Secret High Council should always consist of eight members, all vacancies to be filled by themselves; that she could make neither war nor peace, nor appoint an officer above the rank of colonel, without the consent of the Council; that she could not condemn a noble to death, nor confiscate his property, without a trial; and that she could neither appoint a successor, nor marry again without the approval of the Council. She was also to sign an agreement whereby she would forfeit the crown "in case of my ceasing to observe these engagements." The Council also decided upon moving the capital back to Moscow.

This might have been the beginning of a more liberal

government for Russia, since it diminished the power of the czar and the people would have benefited by the increased rights of the nobles, as was the case in England. It was the nobility who objected, from fear that the power might be absorbed in the families of the Council members. Anne of Courland accepted the conditions and came to Moscow. There she received letters from the enemies of the Council imploring her to disregard her promises. On the 25th of February, 1731, the Council was in session when an officer appeared summoning them before the czarina. Upon arrival in the apartment, they found about eight hundred persons presenting a petition that Anne might restore autocracy. She read it and seemed astonished: "What!" she exclaimed, "the conditions sent to me at Mittau were not the will of the people?" There was a shout of "No! no!" "Then," she said, addressing the Council, "you have deceived me!" Anne was a true daughter of the czars. She began by exiling the principal members of the Council to their estates; when she saw that there was no opposition, they were sent to Siberia; and when no one remonstrated, other members were condemned to a cruel death.

Anne was thirty-five years old when she was crowned as czarina. She had been in Germany so long that she preferred to surround herself with Germans who did serve her well, but they naturally aroused the jealousy and hatred of the Russian nobles. In 1733, Augustus II, King of Poland, died. Russia, Prussia, and France, each had a candidate. Austria and Russia favored Augustus III of Saxony, and Louis XV of France supported his father-in-law Stanislas Lecszinski.

This candidate secretly proceeded to Warsaw, where he was elected by a vote of 60,000 against 4,000. A Russian army crossed the frontier, whereupon Stanislas withdrew to Dantzig and the Russians proclaimed Augustus III. The war spread and a Russian army of 20,000 men advanced as far as

Heidelberg in Baden. It ended in 1735, by the Peace of Vienna, but Russia became involved in a war with Turkey, as an ally of Austria.

In 1736, the Russians took Azof and ravaged the western Crimea. In the following year they laid waste its eastern part, and in 1739 they gained a great victory at Savoutchani. Austria was not anxious to have Russia as a close neighbor, and arranged the Peace of Belgrade. (1739.) Russia surrendered all the conquests, except a small tongue of land between the Dnieper and the Bug. Sweden threatened war, but it was averted. The following year, 1740, Anne died, leaving the throne to her infant son, Ivan of Brunswick.

Anne Ivanovna introduced western luxury into Russia. Prior to her arrival, fashions were unknown, and people used to wear their clothes until they were worn out. Soon after restoring autocracy, she returned to St. Petersburg where she endeavored to establish a court in imitation of that of France. She could compel her nobles to appear in the costume of the west, and, unless they were very wealthy, make them sacrifice estates and serfs to pay his increased expenses, but of the refinement which creates fashion, there was none. One of her guests, a procurator-general was so intoxicated at one of her receptions that he insulted one of Anne's most trusted advisers; she was a witness, but only laughed heartily.

The young nobles benefited by the German influence at Court, since they received a better education. A law was made requiring them to study from their seventh to their twentieth year, and to serve the government from that age until they were forty-five. Between the age of twelve and sixteen they were made to appear before an examining board, and any one failing to pass the second time in catechism, arithmetic, and geometry, was put into the navy. In the schools for young nobles,—the serfs received no instruction of any kind,—the course of studies was enlarged after the German system.

Anne's infant son, Ivan, was three months old, when he succeeded to the throne as Ivan VI. Elizabeth, the daughter of Peter the Great and Catherine, was twenty-eight years old; tall and masculine, bright and bold, daring on horseback as well as on the water, she had made a host of friends among the high officials and the Guards. She found an able adviser in the French Minister at St. Petersburg who was anxious to destroy the influence of Germany. The Swedes went so far as to begin a war, proclaiming the desire to deliver "the glorious Russian nation" from the German yoke. Elizabeth decided that the time had come to act, when the regiments devoted to her were ordered to the frontier. In the night of October 25, 1741, she went with three friends to the barracks. "Boys," she said to the men, "you know whose daughter I am?" "Matuska," (little mother), they replied, "we are ready; we will kill all of them." She said that she did not wish any blood to be shed, and added: "I swear to die for you; will *you* swear to die for me?" They made the oath. When she returned to the palace, the regent, the infant czar, and the German members of the Government were arrested. Ivan VI was sent to a fortress near the Swedish frontier. The Germans were brought before a court and condemned to death, but Elizabeth commuted the sentence to exile. After this she went to Moscow, where she was crowned as czarina. Her next act was to send for her nephew, Peter, the son of her sister Anne of Holstein. He came and entered the Greek Church, when he was proclaimed as heir to the throne as Peter Feodorovitch.

Sweden demanded the cession of the territory conquered by Peter the Great, and, since Elizabeth refused, the war continued. But Sweden was no longer the kingdom of Charles XII; the Russians were everywhere victorious, and by the Peace of Abo, in 1743, Sweden ceded South Finland and agreed to elect Elizabeth's ally, Adolphus of Holstein, as heir to the throne.

In 1740 the Emperor of Germany died, after obtaining from the powers the consent to set aside the Salic Law of succession, in favor of his daughter. This law restricted the right of succession to male heirs exclusively. In violation of the pledged word, several claimants appeared to contest the claim of his daughter Maria Theresa, and since almost every nation took sides, it was important to know what Russia would do. Elizabeth was undecided; at least, she played with both sides until 1746, when she entered into an alliance with Maria Theresa, while England promised subsidies in money. It was, however, 1748 before a Russian army of 30,000 men passed through Germany and took up a position on the Rhine. In the same year the war was ended by the Peace of Aix-la-Chapelle, without the Russians having been under fire.

Elizabeth hated Frederick the Great of Prussia. She claimed that "The King of Prussia is certainly a bad prince who has no fear of God before his eyes; he turns holy things into ridicule, and he never goes to church." The real reason was that Frederick had expressed his opinion about Elizabeth's private life, and she was not the woman to forgive his remarks. Then again, Frederick had an excellent army of 200,000 men; Elizabeth's chancellor, on that account, called Prussia "the most dangerous of neighbors, whose power it was necessary to break."

Russia, Austria, France, and Saxony, entered into a secret alliance against Prussia. Frederick found it out, and in 1756, began the famous Seven Years' War. The same year, 83,000 Russians under Apraxine crossed the frontier and seized East Prussia. A battle was fought; the Russians were the victors, but Apraxine fell back across the Niemen. France and Austria suspected treachery; Apraxine was arrested and the chancellor was dismissed and exiled. Fermor was appointed commander-in-chief.

The Russian army recrossed the frontier in 1758, took Koenigsberg and bombarded Kuestrin on the Oder. Frederick with 32,000 men attacked the Russian army 89,000 strong at Zorndorf. The Russians fought stubbornly but were defeated with a loss of 20,000 men. Fermor was recalled, and succeeded by Soltykof who, in 1759, entered Frankfort on the Oder. Another battle was fought and Frederick was defeated by greatly superior numbers. He lost 8,000 men. Prussia was exhausted, but his enemies, too, began to feel the expense of the war. Elizabeth, however, was determined to humble the outspoken King when she died suddenly in 1761. She was succeeded by her nephew Peter Feodorovitch under the name of Peter III.

Elizabeth, although careless in her mode of living, was a stout supporter of the Greek Church. In 1742, she agreed with the Holy Synod to suppress all other churches, as well as the Mosques or Mahomedan temples in the south. This caused a revolt of the Mahomedans. The Jews were also expelled in some parts of the empire. A fever of fanaticism broke out; fifty-three *raskolnik* in Russia, and one hundred and seventy-two in Siberia, burned themselves to death.

Count Ivan Schouvalof, one of Elizabeth's friends, believed in education and was given a free hand. He ordered that the priests and their children should attend school, on penalty of being whipped. He founded the University of Moscow, which has educated many learned Russians. To induce students to enter, he induced Elizabeth to make a law that all students should be tchins of the tenth grade, and the professors hold the eighth grade. He sent young men abroad to study and established higher schools in every Government. Schouvalof was also the founder of the Academy of Fine Arts at St. Petersburg.

That capital was growing; its population was 74,000 under Elizabeth. She built the Winter Palace and saw the plans for Tsarskoe Selo, the magnificent retreat of the Russian emperors. She reestablished the Senate, as organized by Peter the Great.

XXI

RUSSIA UNDER CATHERINE II (THE GREAT)

Peter III was thirty-four years old when he succeeded to the throne. Although it was twenty years since his aunt Elizabeth sent for him from Holstein, he was more of a German than a Russian, and had an intense admiration for Frederick the Great. He at once reversed Russia's policy, ordered the commander-in-chief of the Russian armies to leave his Austrian allies, and made peace with the King of Prussia to whom he restored all Russia's conquests. Then he entered into an alliance with Frederick, which was the means of saving Prussia.

Peter relieved the nobles of the duty of serving the state, for which they were so grateful that they proposed to erect his statue in gold; he heard of it, and forbade their doing so. He abolished the Secret Court of Police, and showed great kindness to the raskols and permitted many of them to return from Siberia. A host of other exiles were recalled, and he thought of relieving the hard lot of the moujiks.

For all this, he was unpopular and disliked. His disregard for old Russian customs and his mode of life gave deep offense. He was married to Sophia of Anhalt, who had assumed the name of Catherine; she was a woman of decided ability and

R. Van Bergen

strong character. Peter wanted a divorce. She heard of it and contrived a conspiracy among the high nobles and officers of the army and navy. Peter had no thought of danger, when he ordered the arrest of Passek, a young officer and favorite of Catherine. Thinking that the conspiracy had been discovered, she left her palace in the outskirts and came to St. Petersburg where the three regiments of Foot Guards declared in her favor, and Peter's uncle was arrested by his own regiment of Horse Guards. When Catherine entered the Winter Palace, she was sure of the army and navy; Cronstadt was seized by her supporters, and she issued a proclamation assuming the government. At the head of 20,000 men, she marched upon the Palace, where the czar, her husband, was residing.

Peter fled to Cronstadt and sought the Admiral. "I am the czar," he said. "There is no longer a czar," was the reply, and all Peter could do was to return to his palace, where he abdicated "like a child being sent to sleep," as Frederick the Great expressed it. He then called on his wife, "after which," Catherine tells us, "I sent the deposed emperor, under the command of Alexis Orlof accompanied by four officers and a detachment of gentle and reasonable men, to a place called Ropcha, fifteen miles from Peterhof, a secluded spot, but very pleasant." Four days later Peter III was dead. Catherine declared that he died of colic "with the blood flying to the brains."

But one was living with just and strong claims to the throne. Ivan VI, the infant czar sent to prison by Elizabeth in 1741, was now twenty-one years old. It was reported that he had lost his reason, which may have been true or false. Catherine disposed of him. She said: "It is my opinion that he should not be allowed to escape, so as to place him beyond the power of doing harm. It would be best to tonsure him (that is, to make a monk of him), and to transfer him to some monastery, neither too near nor too far off; it will suffice if it does not become a shrine." She did not desire that the people should make a martyr of a descendant of Peter the Great, while she, a foreign woman, was occupying the throne. Poor Ivan was murdered by his keepers two years later, when a lieutenant of the Guards was trying to effect his escape. After that, Catherine had no rival for the crown, except her son Paul, whom she disliked.

At first it seemed as if Catherine would reverse her husband's policy with regard to Prussia. She gave orders to the army to leave the Prussian camp, but she did not command active hostilities; since the parties felt the exhaustion of a seven years' struggle, peace negotiations were begun and concluded successfully.

Catherine made Russia a party to the System of the North; that is, she entered into an alliance with England, Prussia, and Denmark, as against France and Austria. Nearly all Europe was deeply interested in the severe illness of the King of Poland, because of the election which must follow his death. Unhappy Poland was bringing destruction upon itself. A lawless nobility kept the country in anarchy, and religious persecution, which had disappeared elsewhere, was still rampant. It was the gold distributed by interested powers, that controlled the vote of the Diet, and since it was merely a question of the highest bidder, Frederick the Great and Catherine came to an understanding. They decided to elect Stanislas Poniatowski, a Polish noble. France and Austria supported the Prince of Saxony, who was also the choice of the Court party. After the death of Augustus III, the Diet assembled and elected the French and Austrian candidate. Members of the Diet asked for Russian intervention and, supported by Catherine's army, Poniatowski was placed on the throne.

Russia and Prussia were not satisfied; they wanted part of the

R. Van Bergen

kingdom and the prevailing anarchy on their frontiers justified them. But Catherine made a pretext out of Poland's religious intolerance,—although the same existed in Russia. In 1765, Koninski, the Bishop of the Greek Church presented to the King a petition asking redress for a number of grievances which he enumerated. The King promised relief and submitted the matter to the Diet of 1766. The majority would not hear of any tolerance, although Russia had on the frontier an army of 80,000 men ready to invade Poland. The Diet of 1767 showed the same foolish spirit, but it was broken when two of its members, both Catholic bishops, were arrested under Russian orders, and carried into Russian territory. The Diet did not appear to resent this violation of a friendly territory but entered in 1768 into a treaty with Russia, in which it was agreed that Poland would make no change in its constitution without Russia's consent. The Russian army was withdrawn from Warsaw, and a deputation from the Diet was sent to St. Petersburg to thank Catherine.

Two hostile parties soon appeared in arms. The Catholics raised the banner "Pro religione et libertate!"—as if they understood what liberty meant! France helped with money, and urged the Sultan of Turkey to declare war against Russia, so that Catherine would be compelled to withdraw her troops. Russia was inciting those of the Greek and Protestant religions to whom assistance was promised.

In the winter of 1768, the Tartars of the Crimea, aided by the Turks, invaded Russia, and Catherine dispatched an army of 30,000 men,—all she could spare. In the following year, the Russians attacked and defeated the enemy 100,000 strong at Khotin on the Dnieper, and in 1770 the Khan of the Crimea met the same fate. In the same year at the battle of Kagul, 17,000 Russians defeated 150,000 Turks commanded by the Grand Vizier. In the same year the Russians destroyed the

Turkish fleet in the port of Chesme. In 1771, the Tartars of the Crimea were put to rout, and the Russians took Bessarabia and some forts on the Danube. They were, however, too late to take possession of the Dardanelles, which the Turks had put into a state of defense.

Austria was becoming alarmed at Russia's victories, and lent a willing ear to the suggestion of Frederick the Great that it would be safer to permit Russia to gain territory belonging to Poland, provided Austria and Prussia should receive their share. On February 17, 1771, a treaty was concluded between Russia and Prussia, and accepted by Austria in April, whereby Poland was deprived of a good part of its territory. Catherine, secured White Russia with a population of 1,600,000; Frederick the Great took West Prussia with 900,000 inhabitants, and Austria received Western Gallicia and Red Russia with 2,500,000 people. This was the beginning of the end of Poland.

The peace negotiations with Turkey were broken off, and war was resumed. Being busy elsewhere, Catherine could not prevent a *coup d'etat* in Sweden, which saved that country from the fate of Poland. Besides suffering from these constant wars, Russia was visited by the plague, which in July and August, 1771, daily carried off a thousand victims in Moscow alone. The Archbishop, an enlightened man, was put to death by a mob for ordering the streets to be fumigated. Troops were necessary to restore order.

The condition of the country was dreadful. Alexander Bibikof was sent to suppress a dangerous insurrection, he wrote to his wife after arriving on the spot, that the general discontent was frightful. It was for this reason that Catherine concluded peace with the sultan in 1774; besides an indemnity, she received Azof on the Don and all the strong places in the Crimea, and was recognized as the protector of the sultan's Christian subjects. In 1775, she finally broke the power of the Cossacks.

Through the mediation of France and Russia, a war between Prussia and Austria concerning the succession in Bavaria, was narrowly averted. During the American War of Independence, Russia, Sweden, Denmark, Prussia, and Portugal, proclaimed armed neutrality, and Holland declared war, because British warships caused endless trouble to vessels under neutral flags. This celebrated act declared "that contra-band goods" included only arms and ammunition. Most countries agreed to this, with the exception of England.

In 1775 Catherine annexed the Crimea, on the plea that anarchy prevailed. Turkey protested and threatened war but France meditated and the sultan recognized the annexation by the Treaty of Constantinople in 1783.

In 1787, a remarkable secret agreement was signed between Russia and Austria. It is known as the *Greek Project*, and was nothing less than a scheme to divide Turkey between the two powers. The plot as proposed by Russia, was to create an independent state under the name of Dacia, to embrace Moldavia, Wallachia, and Bessarabia, with a prince belonging to the Greek Church at the head. Russia was to receive Otchakof, the shore between the Bug and the Dnieper, and some islands in the Archipelago, and Austria would annex the Turkish province adjoining its territory. If the Turk should be expelled from Europe, the old Byzantine Empire was to be reestablished, and the throne occupied by Catherine's grandson Constantine, "who would renounce all his claims to Russia, so that the two empires might never be united under the same scepter." Austria agreed on condition that she should also receive the Venetian possessions in Moldavia, when Venice would be indemnified by part of Greece.

Soon after this the sultan declared war against Russia. This took Catherine by surprise. Other enemies sprang up: the King of Prussia wanted Dantzig, the King of Sweden, South Finland. The latter invaded Russia and might have marched upon St. Petersburg, for all Catherine could collect was an army of 12,000 men. A mutiny in the camp of Gustavus III, compelled him to return to Stockholm, and the opportunity was lost. He defeated the Russians in the naval battle of Svenska Sund, but a second engagement was to the advantage of Russia. The French Revolution caused him to make peace, and to enter into an alliance with Russia against the French.

In the south Russian arms were more fortunate. The Turks were defeated in 1789, and 1790, on which occasions a young general named Souvorof distinguished himself. Upon the death of Joseph II of Austria, his successor Leopold made peace with Turkey at Sistova. (1791.) It was the French revolution, which seriously alarmed every crowned head in Europe, and which induced Catherine to follow Leopold's example at Jassy, in January, 1792, Russia kept only Otchakof and the shore between the Bug and the Dniester.

Poland, meanwhile, had made an earnest effort at reform. Thaddeus Kosciusko had returned from the United States, where he had fought for liberty and was trying to save his own country. Born in 1752, he entered a military school founded by the Czartoryskis at the age of twelve, and distinguished himself by attention to his studies and duties. His father was assassinated by exasperated peasants, and he himself was scornfully ejected by a powerful noble whose daughter he was courting. Attracted by the struggle of a handful of colonists against powerful England, he went to

America and served with distinction in the War of the Revolution. After seeing Great Britain humbled and a new republic established in the New World, he came back to Poland and was soon among the foremost reformers,—a man in whom the patriotic Poles justly trusted. But traitors were found to accept Russian bribes, and for the second time Poland was despoiled. Russia annexed the eastern provinces with 3,000,000 inhabitants, and Prussia took Dantzig and Thorn. Austria was told that she might take from the French Republic as much as she wished,—or could.

Manfully and indefatigably did Kosciusko labor to stem the tide of his country's ruin. His patriotism aroused even that of the poor, down-trodden serfs, who had no interests to defend, yet stood by him in battle when the nobles on horseback fled, and wrenched a victory out of defeat. Well might Kosciusko thereafter dress in the garb of a peasant; a gentleman's dress was a badge of dishonor.

It was in 1794, that this battle took place and gave the signal, too, for an effort to restore Poland. But Austria, Prussia, and Russia combined, and Poland was lost. Heroic children were made to pay for the sins of their fathers. Poland expired in 1795. Prussia took Eastern Poland, including Warsaw; Austria annexed Cracow, Sandomir, Lublin, and Selm, and Russia took what remained. The patriots dispersed; most of them took service with the French, hoping for an opportunity to revive their country.

Catherine took especial pains to prevent the ideas, which alone made the French revolution possible, from entering into Russia. There was no occasion for this prudence. The great majority of the Russian people did not know of any world beyond Russia; most of them knew nothing beyond the narrow horizon of their own village, and could neither read nor write. The harrowing tales brought by the fugitive

French nobles did not tend toward inspiring the Russian aristocracy with sympathy for Liberty, Equality, and Fraternity.

Satisfied that Russia was beyond the sphere of what she regarded as pernicious doctrines, Catherine determined to make the greatest possible profit out of the disturbed condition of Europe. She never ceased to incite Prussia and Austria against the French Republic, but carefully refrained from spending a dollar or risking a man. She pleaded first her war with Turkey, and afterwards the Polish insurrection. She said to Osterman, one of her ministers: "Am I wrong? For reasons that I cannot give to the Courts of Berlin and Vienna, I wish to involve them in these affairs, so that I may have my hands free. Many of my enterprises are still unfinished, and they must be so occupied as to leave me unfettered."

While Europe was engaged in the hopeless task of establishing and maintaining the divine rights of kings, Catherine began a war with Persia. One of her "unfinished enterprises" was interrupted by her death in November, 1796, at the age of sixty-seven. She left the throne to her son Paul.

XXII

RUSSIA DURING THE WARS OF NAPOLEON

Paul was forty-two years old when he succeeded to the throne. His youth and early manhood had been far from pleasant. His mother had never shown any love for him, and Paul had not forgotten his father's sudden death. He was held in absolute submission, and was not permitted to share in the government; he had not even a voice in the education of his children. The courtiers, in order to please his mother, showed him scant courtesy; this is probably the reason of his sensitiveness after he came to the throne. He ordered men and women to kneel down in the street when he was passing, and those who drove in carriages had to halt. It is also shown in this remark, "Know that the only person of consideration in Russia is the person whom I address, at the moment that I am addressing him." It was justice, but it reflected upon his mother's memory when, immediately after her death, Paul ordered his father's remains to be exhumed, to be buried at the same time and with the same pomp as those of Catherine.

Such a man could have no sympathy with the French revolution which was shaking the foundations of Old Europe. He forbade the use of any word that might be construed to refer to it. He ordered the army to adopt the Russian uniform, including the powdered pigtails of that time. Souvorof fell in disgrace because he was reported to have said: "There is powder and powder. Shoe buckles are not gun carriages, nor pigtails bayonets; we are not Prussians but Russians."

Paul pardoned a number of exiled Poles, and brought the last king, Stanislas Poniatowski, to St. Petersburg. He discontinued the war with Persia, and instructed his ambassadors to announce that since Russia, and Russia alone, had been at war since 1756, "the humanity of the Emperor did not allow him to refuse his beloved subjects the peace for which they sighed."

Nevertheless, Russia was drawn into Napoleon's gigantic wars. Uneasy at the plans of the French Republic, Paul entered into an alliance with England, Austria, Naples, and Turkey. He furnished troops for England's descent upon Holland, and recalled Souvorof to take command of the Russian forces cooperating with those of Austria. The British expedition proved a failure, but Souvorof's strategy and indomitable courage shed glory upon the Russian army.

When Souvorof arrived at Vienna, he took command of the allied forces consisting of 90,000 men. On April 28, 1799, he surprised Moreau at Cassano and took 3,000 prisoners. He entered Milan, and soon after laid siege to Mantua, Alessandria, and Turin. On June 17, Souvorof was attacked on the Trebia; the battle lasted three days, leaving the victory to the Russians. After the victory at Novi, on the 15th of August, the French were forced to evacuate Italy.

Souvorof had divided his force of 80,000 Russians into two corps, one to operate in Switzerland, the other under his own command, to conduct the campaign in Italy. His great success brought upon him the envy of the Austrian generals, by whom his movements were constantly hampered. He therefore resolved to effect a junction with the forces in Switzerland, who, on the 26th of September, had been defeated at Zurich with a loss of 6,000 men. Souvorof did not know this. He reached the St. Gothard on the 21st and crossed it under unheard-of difficulties. "In this kingdom of terrors," he writes to Paul, "abysses open beside us at every step, like tombs awaiting our arrival. Nights spent among the clouds, thunder that never ceases, rain, fog, the noise of cataracts, the breaking of avalanches, enormous masses of rocks and ice which fall from the heights, torrents which sometimes carry men and horses down the precipices, the St. Gothard, that colossus who sees the mists pass under him,— we have surmounted all, and in these inaccessible spots the enemy has been forced to give way before us. Words fail to describe the horrors we have seen, and in the midst of which Providence has preserved us." "The Russian, inhabitant of the plain, was awestruck by the grandeur of this mountain scenery."

Souvorof brushed the French out of his way until, on the 26th, he arrived at Altdorf with the loss of only 2,000 men. Here he received information of the defeat at Zurich, and saw that he was surrounded on all sides by superior forces. His retreat showed the highest military skill, as well as the man's indomitable energy. Over untrodden mountains, and snow at one place five feet deep, he guided the remains of his army to a lower altitude, and went into winter quarters between the Iler and the Lech.

Souvorof complained bitterly to the czar of the Austrian generals, who had given him ample reason. At about this time Napoleon had returned from his fruitless campaign in Egypt, and at Marengo defeated the Austrians, whereby the results of Souvorof's campaign were lost. Paul was angry at Austria and Great Britain. Napoleon, shrewdly guessed the czar's feelings, released the Russian prisoners, after equipping them anew. Paul satisfied that Napoleon was an enemy of republican institutions, conceived an intense admiration for his military genius, and came to an understanding with him to overthrow British rule in India. The czar at once commenced to prepare its execution. Two armies were formed; one was to march on the Upper Indus by way of Khiva and Bokhara, while the Cossacks under their hetman Denisof would go by Orenburg. He was confident that the gigantic task could be accomplished, and sent daily instructions to the hetman.

Napoleon had a far better idea of the difficulties, but he did not consider the expedition as hopeless. But even if it failed, he would be the winner, because England would be compelled to send most of her navy to India, while Russia would be too fully occupied, to interfere with his projects in Europe. The Cossacks started on their long journey, by crossing the Volga on the floating ice when, on the 24th of March, 1801, Paul was assassinated in his palace.

There was no doubt as to the guilty men, but Paul's son, Alexander, who succeeded him, did not order an investigation. Pahlen, Panine, Zoubof, and others, known as the "men of the 24th of March," were removed from office, but that was their only punishment. Paul's mother had alienated her grandchildren from the father, and Alexander always showed greater affection for Catherine than for Paul. The greatest sufferer was Napoleon, who saw his grand schemes go up in smoke. Alexander reversed his father's policy, both at home and abroad. He came to an understanding with England. Napoleon tried earnestly to secure the new czar's friendship. He wanted a free hand in Europe and in return offered the same privilege in Asia, but Alexander mistrusted the First Consul. The murder of the Duke of Enghien, who, by Napoleon's order, was kidnaped in a neutral territory and shot,—still further alienated the czar.

After Napoleon's coronation as emperor, Alexander entered into an alliance with England, whereby he would receive six million dollars for every 100,000 men Russia placed in the field. The Emperor of Austria and the King of Prussia joined, but the Austrians, whose generals seemed unable to learn by experience, were defeated before the Russian army could reach the Tyrol. Once again the Russians covered themselves with glory by Koutouzof's masterly retreat to the north, and Bagration's heroic self-sacrifice. At Olmutz, in the presence of Alexander, the Russo-Austrian army, 80,000 strong, was attacked by Napoleon with 70,000 men. The Austrians had induced the czar to adopt their plan of battle, and it met with the usual result. Alexander escaped, escorted by his physician, two Cossacks, and a company of the Guards. (Dec. 2., 1805.) Twenty-four days later Alexander concluded peace with France by the Treaty of Presburg.

The growing power of Napoleon induced Alexander to enter into a new coalition with England, Prussia, and Sweden. Russia bore the brunt of the war, after Prussia had been rendered harmless after the battles of Jena and Auerstadt. The Russians withdrew from Prussian Poland; they suddenly left their winter quarters and attacked the French. On the 8th of February, one of the bloodiest battles was fought at Eylau; the French claimed the victory, but it was barren of results.

Napoleon dreaded Russia. He persuaded the Sultan of Turkey and the Shah of Persia to declare war, so as to occupy Alexander elsewhere. The czar, however, was loyal to his allies until, on the 14th of June, his army was almost annihilated at Friedland. This loss compelled him to enter into negotiations. On June 25, 1807, the two emperors met on a raft at Tilsit. Napoleon was prepared to do almost anything that would induce Alexander to cease interfering in Europe. An offensive-defensive alliance was concluded, whereby Napoleon agreed not to oppose the expulsion of the

Turk or Russia's conquest of Constantinople. The czar meant to carry out the treaty in letter and in spirit, but he soon saw that Napoleon's ambition was limitless, and that he was playing with his ally. This was evident by the proposed partition of Turkey: nothing came of it. Still he accepted Napoleon's invitation to a conference at Erfurt, where he was received by the French Emperor amid a court composed of sovereigns and princes. A convention was signed on the 12th of October, 1808, whereby Alexander promised Napoleon a free hand, in return for the annexation by Russia of Finland and the Turkish provinces on the Danube.

This led to a war with Great Britain, Sweden, and Austria, not including Turkey and Persia. Russia acquired Finland, when Alexander, after convoking the Diet, guaranteed its constitution, privileges, and university. In 1809, war again broke out between Austria and France. By the terms of the alliance, Russia had agreed to furnish troops, but they showed that they did not relish fighting with the French. There were two engagements; in one of these, the casualties were one Russian killed and two wounded. By an oversight of Napoleon the Poles serving under him were to cooperate with the Russians, and, far from doing so, they often came to blows. The Russian general constantly sent complaints to the czar. Napoleon made a great effort to appease Alexander by assigning to Russia Eastern Gallicia with a population of 400,000. Alexander declined to be represented in the peace negotiations at Vienna. Napoleon's creation of the Grand Dukedom of Warsaw was a constant menace to Russia.

Meanwhile the Russians were uniformly victorious in Turkey; the czar concluded peace only when it was evident that war with France was unavoidable, and that Russia would need every man. It was on this account that he gave easy terms to the hard-pressed Sultan. Russia annexed Bessarabia, part of Roumania, Ismail, and Kilia on the Lower Danube.

R. Van Bergen

The time for the momentous struggle had arrived. Napoleon, the master of Continental Europe, thought that he was more than a match for serf-ridden Russia. He reckoned upon the echo which the words liberty, equality, and fraternity, would awaken in the hearts of the moujik, and forgot that they were abstract ideas which to the serf, struggling for enough black bread to allay the cravings of hunger, were so many empty sounds. He tried to arouse Europe's suspicions of Russia's designs, not thinking that any yoke, even that of the Tartars, would be a welcome relief to nations mourning for the slaughter of their sons.

Napoleon left Paris for Dresden on the 9th of May, 1812; on the first of June an army of 678,000 men, including 60,000 Poles, stood ready to invade Russia. Alexander had only 150,000 men under Bagration and Barclay de Tolly, 90,000 posted on the Niemen, and 60,000 on the Vistula; but he issued a proclamation announcing a Holy War. "Rise all of you!" he urged, "With the Cross in your hearts and arms in your hands, no human force can prevail against you!"

Napoleon advanced clutching shadows. After his army left Wilna, leaving dead desolation in its wake, the time soon came when retreat was no longer possible. Russian patriotism clamored for battle and Russian prudence had to give way to it. All of Koutouzof's remarkable influence was required to restrain his men under the retreat which foretold victory, because every step forward sealed Napoleon's doom. The Corsican knew it but, with the superstition born in him, trusted to his star. Finally he drew near Moscow, the Holy City, where Count Rostopchine, the governor, was preparing the grand climax of the drama, while pacifying Russian patriotism by a series of hardy falsehoods. "I have resolved," he explained, "at every disagreeable piece of news to raise doubts as to its truth; by this means, I shall weaken the first impression, and before there is time to verify it, others will come which will require investigation." The people implicitly believed his most daring inventions. When he evacuated Moscow, he ordered all prisons to be opened, and the guns in the arsenal to be distributed among the people; he also had the pumps removed and finally gave instructions to set fire to the stores of *vodka* and the boats loaded with alcohol.

Napoleon arrived at the Kremlin on the 14th of September. Short as was his sojourn, it was with difficulty that he escaped through the flames and found refuge in a park. Why did he waste thirty-five days in the charred capital? Was it belief in his star, or was it despair at the ruin of his prospects? On the 13th of October, the remnant of the Grand Army started on its long journey over the desert it had left behind, because all other roads were closed to it. The retreat has been described by many writers; but what pen shall do justice to the suffering caused by the unusually severe winter, the snow, the ice, the hunger, and the thirst? And how many hearts were rent, when the news came of the dead, the wounded, and the missing? Napoleon's campaign in Russia was the most impressive sermon against war, but it fell upon heedless ears.

After the Battle of the Berezina, Napoleon left the army and hurried home. All his thoughts were on the effect of the disastrous defeat,—not upon the hundred thousand desolate homes, but upon his own fortunes. He arrived in Paris where he gathered 450,000 men, many of them mere youths, to support him with their blood. But Europe was weary of slaughter. Kings might tremble for their crowns, it was the people, aroused to frenzy, that impelled them to action. On Napoleon's heels, besides, there was a bloodhound whom nobler instincts than mere self-preservation inspired to ceaseless pursuit. Alexander I, at this time, earned and deserved the glorious surname of The Well-beloved. Not a thought of self-glory or personal aggrandizement sullied the relentless chase. Emperors and kings dreading the awakened conscience of the people would have made peace, and they could have done so with security for themselves, but Alexander said, "No!" Under fire at the four days' battle of Leipzig, he personally directed reenforcements where they were required. And when, at last, the host of invaders stepped on the soil whose people during twenty years had committed outrages in almost every known country of Europe, they were noble words which the Autocrat addressed to his troops whom he had brought so far away from home. "By invading our empire," he says, "the enemy has done us much harm, and has therefore been subjected to a terrible chastisement. The anger of God has overthrown him. Do not let us imitate him. The merciful God does not love cruel and inhuman men. Let us forget the evil he has wrought; let us carry to our foes, not vengeance and hate, but friendship, and a hand extended in peace."

These were not mere words; Alexander the Well-beloved was sincere. But it was he who refused to receive Napoleon's envoy at Freiburg, and it was he who, when Napoleon, fighting like a tiger at bay, was defeating the separated armies, so that the British envoy urged to come to terms with him, answered, "It would not be a peace but a truce. I cannot come four hundred leagues to your assistance every day. No peace, so long as Napoleon is on the throne!" By his direction the united armies rolled like an avalanche upon Paris,—and Napoleon gave up the struggle by abdicating.

Again it was Alexander the Well-beloved who intervened when other powers would have overwhelmed the fallen colossus. It was Alexander who procured for his enemy the sovereignty of the island of Elba, and commissioned Count Schouvalof to escort him. "I confide to you a great mission;" he said; "you will answer to me with your head for a single hair which falls from the head of Napoleon."

At the Congress of Vienna assembled the statesmen to dispose of nations and peoples, as their own ambition prompted. Alexander desired to unite Poland to his crown, but separate from Russia; but was opposed by Austria, Great Britain, and France, who entered into a secret alliance against him. Had Napoleon waited two hundred days instead of half that time, who knows that he might not yet have been the arbiter of Europe? His descent united all factions, and Alexander declared that he would pursue Napoleon "down to his last man and his last ruble."

Once again armies were set in motion, and once again Napoleon resorted to his well-known tactics of destroying his enemies one by one. He failed at Waterloo. (June 17, 1815.) Again the allies re-entered Paris, the Prussians first but closely followed by the czar and his army.

"Justice, but no revenge!" proclaimed Alexander when Bluecher would have followed Napoleon's example of robbing a country of its works of art. The czar stood the friend of France when Prussia demanded a frontier which would render her safe from French invasion; but he said frankly that he "wished to allow some danger to exist on that side, so that Germany, having need of Russia, might remain dependent," He was in favor of allowing the French to select their own government, but was overruled. At last the allies came to an understanding, and Poland was joined to the Russian Crown.

The Polish soldiers who had fought so bravely under Napoleon, placed themselves at the czar's service, hoping and trusting that their country would revive under a Russian king. Alexander's promises at Vienna had been vague, but recent events had made a deep impression upon him. In this frame of mind, he directed that Poland be restored. This was announced on the 21st of June, at Warsaw amid the roar of cannon. Constantine, Alexander's brother, was made King, and a legislative body, composed of a senate and house of representatives, was formed under a constitution which also guaranteed the freedom of the press.

Thus Alexander returned to Russia. Soon after that he gave evidence that strong emotions were required to subdue the inborn prejudice in favor of autocracy. Russia, of necessity, had acquired an overwhelming influence in Europe. This showed at the several Congresses, at Aix-la-Chapelle in 1818, at Carlsbad in 1819, at Troppau in 1820, and at Verona in 1822. The crowned heads of Europe appeared unable to comprehend that the French revolution, with its orgies of blood and tears, had produced an impassable abyss between the eighteenth and nineteenth centuries. They wished to return to the conditions prevailing before the revolution, which caused the success of that upheaval; but the people, the masses, had quaffed of the cup of liberty, and the taste lingered. The Holy Alliance with its unholy aims might ordain what it pleased, the *people* obstinately refused to resume the place of beasts of burden for the benefit of the State. Thus a spirit of unrest was perceptible, and when Alexander learned that his "I, the czar, will it!" was not able to restore quiet, he joined the other crowned heads in their struggle against more liberal ideas. From that time his conduct changed.

There was evidence of this in the events occurring in the south. The majority of the inhabitants of the Balkan provinces of Turkey belonged to the Greek Church, and looked to Alexander for relief from the oppressive Mahomedan yoke. The Servians took up arms, the people of Greece did the same. On Easter day, 1821, the Patriarch of the Greek Church at Constantinople was seized at the altar, and hung in his vestment at the door of the church. Three metropolitans and eight bishops were also murdered. The news caused deep indignation in Russia, but Alexander moved not. He believed in the theory that no people should be encouraged in rising against its ordained masters. In Russia all liberal ideas were rigidly suppressed.

In 1825, Alexander left St. Petersburg for the south where he intended to spend some time. He was full of gloomy forebodings and gave further evidence of an unsound mind by having a mass for the dead sung in his presence in broad daylight. While in the Crimea he was heard to repeat: "They may say what they like of me, but I have lived and will die a republican." He died on the 19th of November, 1825, while on his journey.

He left no sons. His brother Constantine had renounced the crown when he became King of Poland, and in 1823, Alexander had made his next brother Nicholas his successor. Alexander's reign marked a new era for Russia inasmuch as it was brought into closer contact with Europe, and promised to change in thought and impulse, from an Asiatic into a European nation. The necessity of securing the help of the masses against Napoleon's invasion created newspapers, and writers of unusual ability expressed their patriotic thoughts in prose and poetry. In 1814, the Imperial Library was opened to the public at St. Petersburg. It contained at that time 242,000 volumes, and about 10,000 manuscripts.

In 1803, Captains Krusenstern and Lisianski made the first Russian voyage around the world in the *Nadejda* (the *Hope*), and the *Neva*. It was on this occasion that Russia entered into relations with the United States.

XXIII

AN EVENTFUL PERIOD

Alexander's will came as a surprise upon Nicholas, but Constantine was loyal to his promise and after a brief but generous contest, Nicholas was crowned at Moscow. Twenty-three days had elapsed since Alexander's death, long enough to show that the spirit of unrest had penetrated into Russia. On the 26th of December there were some disturbances at Moscow, but they were suppressed without great trouble. The secret police hunted down the leaders, many of whom were known in art or literature, but they suffered death. Nicholas, a man of colossal stature, commanding appearance, iron will, passion for a military life, of simple and correct habits, was a true champion of the right divine of kings. He had neither sympathy nor patience with any movement tending toward greater liberty for the people. Nevertheless Nicholas was much more popular than Alexander had been, because he was the type of the Russian czars, who had increased Russia's power and territory.

Not many days after his coronation, Nicholas became involved in a quarrel with the Shah of Persia. In vain did the shah call upon Great Britain for help; the Persians were twice defeated in 1826, and the Russians were on the road to Teheran when the shah preferred to save his capital by ceding two provinces, and paying a heavy indemnity in 1828. The following year, the Russian Minister at Teheran was murdered, but Persia escaped with a humble apology.

Turkey, too, was made to feel Nicholas' heavy hand; urged by other powers the sultan submitted to the loss of territory in Asia, which had been in dispute, and permitted the free passage of Russian vessels between the Black Sea and the Mediterranean. (Convention of Akkerman, Oct. 8, 1826.) The czar, after this, took up the Greek question, and entered into an agreement with England and France. In vain did the sultan offer the plea which had been successful with Alexander, that the Greeks "violated the passive obedience owed by subjects to their legitimate sovereigns." Nicholas wanted Turkey for himself, and proposed to leave no stone unturned to secure possession of Constantinople.

After the battle of Navarino, on the 20th of October, 1827, where the allied forces destroyed the Turkish fleet. England withdrew, suspicious of Nicholas' schemes; but France and Russia continued the war until by the Peace of Adrianople, the sultan recognized the independence of Greece,—and ceded to Russia four fortresses in Asia and the islands in the delta of the Danube. Russia was thus in possession of the whole southern slope of the Caucasus, besides holding part of its northern front. The czar began war upon the tribes dwelling in the mountains, but found that he had engaged in a very difficult enterprise. A soldier-priest named Schamyl defied the power of Russia for a quarter of a century. It cost Nicholas more in men and money to subdue the liberty-loving mountaineer, than all the wars he waged in Asia.

The year 1830, was one of great unrest in Europe. Nicholas was deeply angered when his friend Charles X of France was expelled. The revolution in Paris was the signal for a similar movement in the capital of Poland. Owing to the independent expression of opinion in the Diet, Alexander had adjourned that body indefinitely in 1822. At the same time the liberty of the press was revoked and the police assumed a power in defiance of the law. The Grand Duke Constantine was really a friend of Poland, but he was eccentric and impetuous and often unconsciously gave offense. In 1830, Nicholas came to Warsaw to open the Diet, when its members made demands which he could not grant. Both sides were angry when Nicholas returned to St. Petersburg.

As soon as the French tricolor was raised above the consulate at Warsaw, the trouble commenced. Taken unprepared, Constantine withdrew with his troops. Again the Poles were divided; the patriots advised reconciliation with Russia, while hotheads demanded the abdication of the Romanofs. The first party sent a deputation to St. Petersburg and another to Paris and London, to secure mediation. The czar's answer was decisive; he absolutely refused to "make concessions (to the revolutionists), as the price of their crimes." Again, too, there was discord among the leaders as they entered upon a life or death struggle. Poland appealed to Europe. The people were sympathetic, but the governments, rejoicing at seeing a revolutionary movement suppressed, refused to interfere.

In February, 1831, a Russian army of 130,000 men invaded Poland. The Poles showed a heroism which appealed to the people of Europe, but more than sympathy was needed to arrest the irresistible Russian advance upon Warsaw. Constantine and the Russian commander-in-chief fell the victims of cholera, but an epidemic of discord struck Poland and sealed its fate. On the 6th of September, Warsaw was invested. The capital was forced to surrender. "Warsaw is at your feet," wrote the commander-in-chief to the czar, who lost no time in trampling upon the conquered. The constitution was abrogated, the Diet, a thing of the past. Poland was no more. Where it had stood, was a Russian province. Russian officials introduced Russian taxes, Russian coinage, and Russian justice such as it was. The Poles saw samples of it when thousands were arrested without process of law, and were sent to prison or to Siberia, while other thousands lost their property by confiscation. In White Russia and Lithuania the use of the Polish language was prohibited and the Catholic Clergy were forced to "ask" admittance to the bosom of the Greek Church. It must be admitted that the Polish peasants benefited by the change. With a view of reducing the influence of the nobles, the government issued regulations protecting the laborer against the landowner.

The Polish revolution caused the reorganization of European policies. Austria and Prussia, each in possession of territory that formerly belonged to Poland, entered into friendly relations with Russia, whereas England and France, where public opinion could not be ignored, drew more closely together. Nicholas was posing as the arbiter of Europe and the champion of kings. He assumed the right to command, but would soon find his will contested.

This was brought home to him in 1832, when trouble broke out between Turkey and Egypt. The Egyptian army was victorious and threatened Constantinople, when the sultan appealed to the powers. Russia responded at once by sending two armies, but a strong protest from England and France caused the withdrawal of the troops of Russia as well as those of Egypt. Baffled, Nicholas on June 3, 1833, entered into an offensive-defensive alliance with the sultan, which really placed Turkey and with it Constantinople in Russia's power. Another sharp protest from England and France prevented the consummation of the alliance.

R. Van Bergen

In 1839 the trouble between Turkey and Egypt recommenced when Great Britain, anxious to preserve Turkey's integrity, entered into an agreement with Russia, Austria and Prussia, which was signed at London in July, 1840. There was some danger of a war with France but England, fearing Russia's designs, returned to her former ally. By the Convention of July 13, 1841, Russia's designs upon old Czargrad were postponed until a more favorable opportunity. In 1844, Nicholas visited England, but his reception in London was cool. He, however, entered into an agreement whereby the Khanates of Central Asia should remain neutral ground between Russia and India.

In 1846, trouble broke out in Gallicia, where the Poles rose against Austria; but as the nobles had to subdue a revolt of their own peasants, order was quickly restored. The free city Cracow was the resort of the Poles. Russia, Austria, and Prussia sent troops against it, and Cracow was annexed by Austria notwithstanding a protest from England and France.

The year 1848 will long be remembered for the blows bestowed upon the divine right of kings, and the privileges which the sovereigns were compelled to concede to the people. The Emperor Ferdinand of Austria was expelled from his capital, and the King of Prussia was subjected to humiliation by his own people. France proclaimed the republic, and Nicholas proclaimed himself the champion of the right divine. He dispatched an army into Hungary, which was soon "at the feet of your Majesty," and felt the wrath of the frightened Ferdinand.

Notwithstanding this cooperation, the understanding among the three powers, Russia, Austria and Prussia, was giving way before individual interests. When, in 1852, Prussia attempted to seize the German provinces of Denmark, it was Nicholas who compelled her to withdraw. On the 8th of May of that year, the independence and integrity of Denmark were recognized by the Treaty of London.

In the same year Louis Napoleon made an end to the French Republic by the notorious *Coup d'Etat*. This gave great satisfaction to the czar who was heard to remark: "France has set an evil example; she will now set a good one. I have faith in the conduct of Louis Napoleon." The new emperor of France did not seem to appreciate this condescension, or else he showed gross ingratitude when France and Austria, without even consulting Nicholas, settled some troubles in Turkey. The czar sent Menzikoff as special envoy to Constantinople to demand a new treaty whereby Russia's rights as Protector of the Greek Christians should be recognized. Supported as he was by France, the sultan refused. Nicholas then had a plain talk with Sir Hamilton Seymour, the British Minister at St. Petersburg, wherein he revealed his designs upon Turkey. As to Constantinople, he said, he might establish himself there as a trustee, but not as a proprietor. Sir Hamilton, as in duty bound, notified his government, and England hastened to join France in opposing Russia.

Pretending that all he wanted was a recognition of his rights, Nicholas, on the 3d of July, 1853, sent an army under Gortchakof across the Pruth. At this an allied British-French fleet took up a position near the threatened point, but did not cross the Straits, which would have been a violation of the treaty. Nicholas stormed; he declared that "This was a threat" and would lead to complications. Austria proposed a conference at which Russia, Great Britain, France, Austria and Prussia assisted. It seemed as if peace would be secured, when the sultan demanded that the Russian forces should withdraw, whereupon Admiral Nakhimof, on the 30th of November, 1853, destroyed the Turkish fleet at Sinope. The British-French fleet then sailed into the Black Sea, and the

R. Van Bergen

Russian ships sought shelter in the ports.

In January, 1854, Napoleon III made a last attempt at maintaining peace, but Nicholas was thoroughly angry at the publication of Seymour's dispatches, claiming that the conversation with the British Minister was entitled to secrecy as between "a friend and a gentleman." Austria and Prussia resented the contempt which the czar had expressed for them, and on the 10th of April England and France entered into an offensive-defensive alliance. Ten days later Austria and Prussia arrived at a written agreement providing for the possibility that the Russians should attack Austria or cross the Balkans. Nicholas had aroused all Europe against him.

The Russian fleet was unable to cope with that of the allies, and thus condemned to inactivity in the ports. After heroic efforts, the Russians were compelled to raise the siege of Silistria, and to retire from the Danube, while Austria occupied the evacuated territory. But Nicholas was dismayed when, after a conference on July 21, 1854, the allied commanders resolved to attack the Crimea. *Russia was unprepared.* It was the assault upon Russia's vaunted "holy soil," which gave a severe blow to the arbiter of Europe, at home as well as abroad. Still with clogged energy the Russians worked to construct defenses. On the 14th of September 500 troopships landed the allied armies, and on the 20th, the Battle of the Alma opened the road to Sebastopol. The port of Balaclava was captured by the allies, and three bloody battles were fought, at Balaclava on the 25th of October, at Inkermann on the 5th of November, and at Eupatoria on the 17th of February, 1855.

It seemed as if the knowledge that an enemy was in Russia, aroused the Russians from a torpor. Pamphlets and other publications denouncing the government in withering terms, seemed to spring up from the pavement. "Arise, Oh Russia!"

says one unknown writer, "Devoured by enemies, ruined by slavery, shamefully oppressed by the stupidity of tchinovnik and spies, awaken from thy long sleep of ignorance and apathy! We have been kept in bondage long enough *by the successors of the Tartar khans*. Arise! and stand erect and calm before the throne of the despot; demand of him a reckoning for the national misfortunes. Tell him boldly that his throne is not the altar of God, and that God has not condemned us to be slaves forever."

The feeling among his people was not unknown to Nicholas. Whatever may be said of him, he was not weakling, fool, or hypocrite, and it was no disgrace that he felt as if the ground were giving way under his feet. He was upright and sincere, and had lived up to his convictions. There is no doubt that when these convictions grew dim, his strength vanished. He was heard to exclaim "My successor may do what he will: I cannot change." The sincerity of this man of iron showed in his losing his courage when doubts arose. Life ceased to have any value for him. One day, in February, 1855, while suffering from a severe cold, he went out without his overcoat. To the physician who tried to restrain him, he said: "You have done your duty; now let me do mine!" A serious illness followed, and he sent for his successor to whom he gave some instructions. As a message to his people, and a last cry for sympathy, he dictated the dispatch "The emperor is dying," which was sent to all the large towns of Russia. On the 19th of March, 1855, Nicholas I was dead.

Under his directions wealthy merchants were classified as "chief citizens," which procured for them exemption from poll-tax, conscription, and corporal punishment. They might take part in the assessment of real estate, and were eligible to the offices to which members of the first class were entitled. The same privilege was extended to all who were entitled to the degree of Master of Arts, and free-born and qualified artists. It was he who built the first railway in Russia, by drawing a straight line between Moscow and St. Petersburg. He also joined the Volga and the Don by a canal. His reign is also noted for the progress of Russian literature. The works of Ivan Tourguenief are known throughout the civilized world.

XXIV

ALEXANDER II, THE LIBERATOR

Alexander II was thirty-seven years old when he succeeded to the throne. The war oppressed Russia, and he felt that peace must be concluded. But Russian diplomacy loves the tortuous path. The first proclamation of the czar announced that he promised "to accomplish the plans and desires of our illustrious predecessors, Peter, Catherine, Alexander the Well-beloved, and our father of imperishable memory." It was hoped that this would cause the other powers to propose peace, on account of the expense of the war. Indeed, a conference was proposed and took place at Vienna, but the demands of the allies were not so modest as Russia expected; hence the war continued, and with it the siege of Sebastopol.

The Danube territory was lost to Russia since, on the 2d December 1854, Austria had undertaken to defend it, and Prussia had agreed to help Austria. But Sebastopol was stubbornly defended. In the latter part of August 1855, 874 guns vomited death and destruction upon the doomed city where the Russians lost 18,000 men. The French had dug fifty miles of trenches during the 366 days of the siege, and 4,100 feet of mines before a single bastion. In one day 70,000 bombs and shells were fired into the town. On the 8th of September the assault was ordered, and Sebastopol fell.

R. Van Bergen

Again Russia tried what boasting would effect. Gortchakof declared to whoever chose to believe him that he would not voluntarily abandon the country where Saint Vladimir had received baptism, and the official newspaper announced that the war was now becoming serious, and that Sebastopol being destroyed, a stronger fortress would be built. This meant that Russia was anxious to secure favorable terms. The war had cost 250,000 men, and Russia's credit at home was in a bad condition. Austria offered the basis of an agreement which was accepted by Russia, and on the 25th of February, 1856, a Congress met at Paris. Five days later the Treaty of Paris was signed. Russia renounced the right of protecting the Christians in the Danubian principalities, and restored the delta of that river. The Black Sea was opened to merchant vessels of all nations, but closed to all warships, and no arsenals were to be constructed on its shores. The sultan agreed to renew the privileges of his Christian subjects, but with the understanding that the powers should not find cause to interfere. It was a hard blow to Russia's prestige, and indefinitely postponed the execution of making of Russia the restored Eastern Roman Empire.

Alexander, in many respects, was the opposite of his father; he seemed more like his uncle in his younger days when he earned the surname of Well-beloved. It may be, however, that Alexander was but the executor of his father's instructions, after doubt began to torture him. It is known that Nicholas had seriously considered the emancipation of the serfs. Alexander took it up in earnest. There were two serious difficulties, namely, the compensation to be allowed to the serf owners, and the extent of the soil to be allotted to the serfs. It must be remembered that, although the peasant had become resigned to serve the landowner, his proverb: "Our backs are the owner's, but the soil is our own," showed how stubbornly he held to the conviction that it was his own land which he cultivated, however little profit he derived from his toil. For once the tchinovnik dared not interfere; public opinion had so strongly condemned their incompetence and dishonesty that the Russian official was glad to efface himself; the landowners, on the other hand, showed little enthusiasm. They knew what their revenues were, but not what they would be under altered circumstances.

Soon after the Treaty of Paris had restored peace, Alexander addressed his "faithful nobles" at Moscow, inviting them to consult about the proper measures to be taken with the view to emancipation. When this produced no results, he appointed a Committee, "for the amelioration of the condition of the peasants." The nobles of Poland, seeing what was coming, declared themselves ready to emancipate their serfs. The czar gave his consent and the ukase containing it was sent to all the governors and marshals of the nobility "for your information," and also "for your instruction if the nobles under your administration should express the same intention as those of the three Lithuanian governments."

The press supported the czar, and for that reason was allowed an unusual freedom of expression. The plan was formed to reconstruct and strengthen the national mir. This was favored by a number of large landowners who saw in this plan the beginning of constitutional liberty. The czar directed that committees be appointed to examine the scheme.

There were at this time 47,000,000 serfs, of whom 21,000,000 belonged to private landowners, 1,400,000 were domestic servants, and the rest Crown peasants who possessed greater privileges and enjoyed some degree of self-government. Their local affairs were administered by the mir and an elected council with an elder as executive. They were judged by elected courts, that is juries, either in the mir court or in that of the volost (district).

Forty-six committees composed of 1,336 land and serf-owners, assembled to discuss the future of 22,500,000 serfs and of 120,000 owners. These committees declared in favor of emancipation, but could not agree upon the allowance of acreage or the indemnity to the owners. Another committee of twelve was appointed, presided over by the czar, but there Alexander met considerable passive opposition. The czar made a journey through the provinces, where he appealed to the nobles, warning them that "reforms came better from above than below." After his return another committee superior in authority to the one existing and composed of friends of emancipation was called. Its members, inspired by the czar, drafted laws whereby emancipation was to proceed at once, and stringent laws were made to prevent the free peasant from again becoming a serf, and to make of him a proprietor upon payment of an indemnity. On the 3d of March, 1861, the emancipation ukase was published.

The scheme, as is evident, was fraught with difficulty. A stroke of the pen by the hand of the czar could set free millions of serfs, but all the czar's power stopped short of endowing the serf with the dignity and responsibility, which are the freeman's birthright. For more than a century and a half, the moujik had been a beast of burden, toiling as he was bid, and finding recreation only in besotting himself with strong drink whenever he could find the means to indulge. Mental faculties, save such as are inseparable from animal instinct, had lain dormant; moral perception was limited between the knout on one side, and gross superstition on the other. Could such a being be intrusted with life and property? When the serf, brutalized by generations of oppression, should come to understand that he was free to do as he pleased, and that the hovel where he and his brood were styed was his to do with as he pleased, what could he be expected to do? Would he not seize the opportunity to indulge in his favorite craving, and, having sold his property, swell the army of homeless vagabonds?

The mir was the only means to prevent this, and mir meant serfdom under another name. The landowners disposed of their land, or of so much as was required to support the peasants, not to individuals but to the mir. To indemnify the owners, the mir could secure a loan whereby the debt was transferred from the owner to the government, and the mir was responsible for its payment as well as for the taxes. The moujik, as part of the mir, was responsible to the community for his share of the debt, and was not allowed to leave his village without a written permission from the starost or elder. He was, therefore, in a worse position than before the emancipation because in time of distress it was his lord's interest to support him, whereas after it he had to deal with a soulless government that demanded the taxes regardless of circumstances. The mir might succeed so long as the peasant remained in a state of tutelage; education only could lift him out of this,—but this means was not considered by the government.

But whatever may have been Alexander's intentions, the men charged with their execution had no sympathy with the moujik. The question never occurred to them: How shall we raise the peasant from his degradation? The problem before them was, how he should be made to support the State, as he had done before. The Russian statesmen had no conception of the truth that the wealth of a State is gauged by the prosperity of the people.

As to the serf, he did not consider that a boon had been bestowed upon him. The soil and the hovel were his, descended to him from his forbears! Why, then, should he pay for them? He clung to this idea with all the stubbornness implanted by a sense of justice upon a limited intelligence. It had been hammered into his head that the Little Father at St.

R. Van Bergen

Petersburg was conferring a favor upon him, and this was within his limited conception; but when he heard what the favor was, the only solution which his cunning brain could devise was that the nobles had cheated the czar, or that there had been some juggling with the ukase. Thus grave disturbances occurred. In one district, that of Kazan, 10,000 men rose at the call of the moujik Petrof, who promised them the real article of liberty. Troops were called out and a hundred peasants besides Petrof were shot. Similar disturbances occurred in other provinces. The poor moujik did not know that he was saddled with a debt which neither he nor his children could hope to pay; but he did know that he was charged with a debt which he had not incurred.

Nevertheless, the emancipation was a step forward. Under the liberal impulse then rushing irresistibly over Russia's broad level the upper classes clamored for reforms. They asked for the re-establishment of the douma as the beginning of a constitutional government, but the czar was not prepared to grant this, and he was right because under existing circumstances the peasants would have to be disfranchized,—and there is small choice between an autocracy and an oligarchy.

It is to be regretted that the reforms in the judicial system, introduced by Alexander in the ukases of 1862 to 1865, have since been rescinded. Secret examinations were displaced by open sessions of the courts, and criminal cases were decided by juries; the police was forbidden to examine the accused, which duty was placed into the hands of a qualified judge. Appeals could be taken to a higher court, and the Senate acted as a Supreme Court in the last resort. Apart from this system was the justice of the peace who adjudged ordinary police cases, acted as an arbitrator, and decided civil suits when the amount involved did not exceed 500 rubles ($250). No appeal could be taken in cases involving less than thirty rubles in civil suits, or fifteen rubles or three days' prison in police offenses. If an appeal was taken the case was brought, not before a higher court, but before the collective justices of the peace of the district, whose verdict could be set aside only by the Senate.

The Russian *goubernii*, governments, were divided into districts (*ouiezdi*). The imperial ukase of 1864, created *zemstvos* or district assemblies composed of representatives of the landed proprietors or gentlemen; or rural communes or mirs, and of the towns. These representatives were elected every three years. The assembly appointed an executive committee which is in permanent session, but the zemstvo assembles once a year. Its duties are strictly limited to local affairs, such as keeping roads and bridges in repair; to watch over education and sanitation, to report on the condition of the harvest, and to guard against the occurrence of famine. Above the district zemstvo is the goubernkoe zemstvo or provincial assembly, whose members are elected from the district zemstvos. Its duties embrace the estimate of the provincial budget, and a general supervision over the districts.

Alexander was kindly disposed and meant to do well. He showed it by removing the barriers erected by his father between Russia and western Europe. Foreigners in Russia were granted civil rights, and Russians were allowed to travel abroad. The universities were relieved of restraints and Jews who had learned a trade could settle where they pleased. All these reforms were so many promises of a new era for Russia.

Alexander soon found out that his concessions only served to create demands for more. The trouble began in Poland, where the news of Nicholas' death was received with relief, if not with joy. Great hopes were entertained from the new

R. Van Bergen

czar; besides, the Europe of 1855 was very different from that of 1825: monarchs had learned the lesson that the people possessed inalienable rights. Italy had shaken off the encumbrance of a number of princelings,—and was the better for it; Austria had been compelled to grant self-government to its Hungarian subjects; why, then, should Poland despair of recovering its independence?

It was Poland's greatest misfortune that her best sons were always divided in opinion; many of them, moreover, thought that Poland's cause should command the sacrifices of every people. They forgot that their country owed its downfall to itself and that, whereas people might express their sympathy, it cannot be expected that they shall neglect their own business for the sake of other people. Some of the leaders expected that the czar would grant them self-government, and Alexander might have done so after some time; but others demanded not only independence but that Russia should restore the parts which she had owned for so many years that they had become parts of the empire. The czar dared not grant such a request, because it would have produced a revolution in Russia, besides a war with Austria and Prussia, since those powers owned part of Poland. He was, however, willing to grant important concessions and did so. In February 1863, an insurrection broke out, and Russian troops were dispatched to subdue it. The Russians acted with great cruelty, so that England, France, and Austria protested on the 17th of June. Russia, knowing that Prussia would come to her assistance paid no attention, and in 1866, Russian Poland became a part of Russia. The Russian language displaced the Polish, and Poland is no longer even a name; it is a memory and a warning,—nothing more.

Quite different was Alexander's treatment of Finland. In 1863, he convoked the Diet of that grand dukedom, where nobility and people appreciated the degree of liberty which they enjoyed. The government did not interfere with the national language or religion, but took measures that neither should spread in Russia.

Alexander's concessions raised the expectation of a constitution among those who knew what the word implies, including the students at the universities. These institutions were closed. The provincial zemstvos exceeded their authority. That of Tver demanded the convocation of the three Estates; that at Toula discussed a national assembly. Was it Alexander or his court and ministers who bore the responsibility for the suppressive means that were employed? It may be that the attempts upon his life, by Karakozof in 1866, and by the Pole Berezofski at Paris in 1867, embittered him. But his kindly feeling and love for his people, taken in conjunction with a later event, warrant the belief that he was ignorant.

R. Van Bergen

XXV

GREAT EVENTS DURING ALEXANDER'S REIGN
NIHILISM

Prussia's behavior during the Polish insurrection brought her into a close friendship with Russia. The result was seen when Austria and Prussia, in 1864, invaded the German provinces of Denmark, when Russia prevented intervention, and Denmark lost the two provinces by the Treaty of Vienna, October 30, 1864. Soon after Prussia and Austria quarreled about the spoils. The countries of South Germany supported Austria. War began on June 18, 1866, and little over two months later, on August 23, 1866, it ended by the Peace of Prague, which gave to Prussia Hanover, Schleswig-Holstein, Hesse, Nassau, and the city of Frankfort. Prussia did not annex Wurtemburg in compliment to the czar, who was related to its king by marriage.

If Russia looked carelessly upon Prussia's growth, not so Napoleon III of France. He saw in it a threat, and to offset Prussia's increase of power, tried to secure other territory. It was evident that nothing but a pretext was needed to bring on war. It was found, and Napoleon declared war on July 15, 1870. Once again it was Alexander who protected Prussia on the east, by threatening Austria which would gladly have seized the opportunity to avenge 1866. As a consequence

France had to fight the whole of Germany; and Russia seized the opportunity for repudiating the treaty of Paris of 1856, which forbade the construction of arsenals on the coast of the Black Sea and did not permit any war vessels in it. None of the powers felt any inclination to fight Russia single-handed, but Prussia proposed a conference, which was held at London. The result was that Russia was left free in the Black Sea, but the sultan has the right to close the Dardanelles to warships.

On January 18, 1871, the King of Prussia became German Emperor, and in the following year the Emperor of Russia, the Emperor of Austria, and the German Emperor met at Vienna, with the result that an alliance was concluded among the three powers.

In 1867 Russia resolved to dispose of its possessions on the western hemisphere by selling Alaska, a territory covering 590,884 square miles, to the United States. In the same year a Slavophil Congress was held at Moscow with the czar's approval. The object was said to be to unite all the nations of Slav origin by a bond of friendship; but the real purpose was to bring them under the rule of the czar. This was apparent when it was resolved to send emissaries among the Slavs under Turkish rule. They met with encouragement in Montenegro, Bulgaria, Bosnia, and Herzegovina. General Ignatieff, the Russian ambassador at Constantinople, thought that this might be the means to bring about the longed-for annexation of the old Czargrad. He worked upon the Turkish subjects belonging to the Greek Church, but showed his hand when, under his decision, the Bulgarians were released from the authority of the Patriarch of Constantinople. In 1875, the Bulgarian Christians rose against the Turkish tax-farmers. The revolt was fanned by the Russian emissaries, and it spread to Servia and Montenegro. Ignatieff did not think that the time was ripe and interfered; but he threatened the Sultan

R. Van Bergen

with European intervention and Abdul Aziz granted the insurgents the privileges enjoyed by the Christians in Turkey.

Austria looked with apprehension upon the increasing influence of Russia in Turkey, and suggested drastic reforms in a note addressed to the powers on December 30, 1875. It was approved and presented to the sultan by the five great European powers. Abdul Aziz quietly accepted it. This was not what the Russian Slavophils expected, and they incited the Servians to revolt. A religious insurrection followed which was put down by the Turks with such cruelty that it aroused universal indignation in Europe, especially in Russia. In Constantinople the Turks were indignant at the sultan's evident fear of Ignatieff. The situation became so alarming that Great Britain assembled a fleet in Besika Bay. The triple alliance, Russia, Austria and Prussia, demanded of the sultan an armistice and the execution of reforms under foreign supervision. The situation changed by a revolution in Turkey on May 29, 1876, when Abdul Aziz was assassinated and succeeded by his nephew Murad V.

Russia felt that war was inevitable and approached Austria with proposals to take joint action. The reply was that Austria could not permit the creation of a Slav state on the frontier and that, if any changes were made in the Balkans, Austria must receive compensation. This was admitted by Russia. A number of Russian officers took service in Servia, among them General Chernaiev, who had gained distinction in Central Asia. Montenegro declared war against Turkey on July 2, 1876.

On the 31st of August, of the same year, Sultan Murad V was deposed, and his half-brother became sultan as Abdul Hamid II. Meanwhile the Turks were victorious, and on September, 17, the Servians asked for an armistice.

The reports of Turkish atrocities aroused great indignation in Great Britain; its government was forced to join the other great powers in a note to the sultan demanding reforms. Abdul Hamid made vague promises but when the Servians, trusting to intervention, again took up arms, they were badly defeated and a great number of Russian officers were killed. The czar was forced to interfere. On October 31, he demanded an armistice of six weeks, to which Abdul Hamid replied that he would make it six months. This was declined because it would keep the Servians too long in suspense, and the war continued. In the beginning of November Chernaiev admitted that the Slav cause was lost unless foreign help came.

Alexander was really concerned in seeking a peaceable solution, but his high officers were equally earnest in preventing it. Ignatieff, at Constantinople, was especially active with every means at his disposal. Alexander suggested a European conference but before it assembled he declared publicly at Moscow (Nov. 10), that, anxious as he was to avoid the shedding of Russian blood, he would act alone to support his brethren in race and religion unless the conference brought relief.

The representatives of the powers met at Constantinople on the 5th of December, 1876. The sultan, a man of rare ability and cunning, knew that Turkey's disintegration was discussed in its own capital. He did not object, but made one of the reform party his Grand Vizier, and astonished the world by proclaiming a constitution on December 25.

The conference concluded its deliberations, and presented its conclusions to the sultan who agreed to submit them to the National Assembly, which was to meet in March, 1877. Abdul Hamid was wise. He made the first legislature Turkey ever had,—and he had firmly resolved that it should also be the last,—responsible for whatever might happen. The session was brief, but long enough to refuse the conditions imposed by the powers.

Alexander demanded that the sultan make peace with Montenegro which was declined. On the 24th of April the czar declared war. England protested against Russia's independent action, but 250,000 men crossed the Turkish frontier. The principal incident was the siege and fall of Plevna (July 20—Dec. 10, 1877), under Osman Pasha. The surrender of this brave Turk alarmed England, which, however, did not grant Turkey's appeal for intervention. It was at the battle of Senova, Jan. 9, 1878, when he captured 27,000 prisoners and 43 Krupp guns, that Skobelef won fame. On January 23, Constantinople was at the czar's mercy.

But this awoke England. On February 13, the British fleet passed through the Dardanelles without obtaining the sultan's consent, and thereby ruined Russia's schemes. In vain did its government complain of the violation of the Treaty of Paris; before the czar could make good his threat that he would occupy Constantinople,—the object of the Russian's most fervid hope,—a fleet of British ironclads prevented its consummation.

Peace negotiations were opened at San Stefano, when Russia imposed exaggerated demands which the cunning sultan hastened to grant, convinced that the other powers would prevent their execution. He was right. Great Britain, Austria, and Turkey entered into an alliance. England sent for Indian troops to occupy Malta, and called out the reserves. The war had cost Russia $600,000,000 and 90,000 men, and she was not in a condition to fight the three powers. Thus, for the second time, Czargrad slipped out of Russia's clutches, and each time she owed the disappointment to Great Britain.

The Balkan question was settled at the Congress at Berlin which opened on June 13, 1878, and finished its sessions a month later. Turkey ceded to Russia a part of Bessarabia, and in Asia, Kars, Ardahan, and Batoum. This ending of the war, so different from what was expected by the Slavophils, caused great dissatisfaction in Russia, and the czar dissolved all Slavophil committees. This gained him the dislike of the high officers and of the tchinovnik.

The absurd and dangerous doctrine of nihilism, that is, the destruction of everything that constitutes society, penetrated into Russia by way of Germany. At first it was nothing but a theory, fascinating for young and inexperienced people such as students of the universities who, unless properly guided, are apt to adopt any idea that appeals to the generous sentiments of youth. In 1864, an exile named Bakunin escaped from Siberia, and made his way to London where he secured employment on the *Kolokol* or "Bell," a revolutionary paper published in Russia which was smuggled over the frontier and scattered broadcast in the czar's domains. Under Bakunin's influence this paper became hostile to society, and preached nihilism. In 1869, a Congress of Nihilists was held at Basel, Switzerland; Bakunin proposed to create an International Committee of active workers.

Soon unmistakable signs of trouble appeared in Russia, but the government was on the alert and took strong means of suppression. Nicholas I, the man with the iron will, had sent an average number of 9,000 persons annually to Siberia; this number under Alexander the Liberator increased to from 16,000 to 20,000. Bakunin urged his followers to "go among the people," and a host of young persons, male and female, many of them belonging to the wealthy classes, adopted the life of the moujik in the villages. But the Russian peasant possesses a degree of cunning which shows his dormant intelligence, and suspected the motives of those who said they wanted to benefit him, and this, added to his real affection for the czar, rendered the attempt of the nihilists a failure. The Russian peasant dreads a change in his condition, because experience has taught him that it will end to his disadvantage. In 1876 there were still 2,000,000 peasants who preferred serfdom.

The Turkish war, when the government was occupied elsewhere, afforded an opportunity which was not neglected by the nihilists. On a July night of the year 1877, fifteen young men met in the forest near Litepsk, and formed a conspiracy against all existing institutions. Two papers, *The Popular Will* and *The Black Partition* advised assassination as the means to gain their object. We may judge of conditions in Russia from knowing that many good and wealthy people made contributions, well aware that arrest and punishment would follow if the secret police should hear of it. In October, 1877, 253 nihilists were arrested, and 160 were convicted at the trial. In February, 1878, General Trepof, Governor of St. Petersburg was openly accused in the papers of gross cruelty toward a prisoner, and Vera Zazulich, a young woman, sought to kill him. She was arrested, tried,—and acquitted, much to the disgust of the authorities who made every effort to re-arrest her. Then began a reign of terror. Officials were condemned to death by an "Executive Committee," composed of members whose names were unknown. The police did not know whom to suspect, and therefore suspected everybody, and no one was safe. Often the condemned officer was warned of his doom by letter or paper, but the messenger could not be found. In April, the president of the Kief University was dangerously wounded, and a police officer was stabbed in public. In August, General Mezensof, Chief of the dreaded Secret Police, was killed, and when the government abolished trial by jury in favor of a military court, it seemed as if the public took the part of the terrorists. These men grew bolder. On the 22d of February, 1878, Prince Krapotkine, the Governor of Kharkof, was shot, and his death sentence was found posted in many cities. On the following 7th of March, Colonel Knoop of the Odessa police, was killed, and as a climax, on the 14th of April a school-teacher named Solovief fired a pistol at the czar. Not satisfied with assassination, the terrorists resorted to incendiarism at Moscow, Nishni Novgorod, and other cities, and there were riots at Rostof. In April, 1878, the government proclaimed martial law, and the most renowned generals, Melikof, Gourko, Todleben, and others were appointed governors with unlimited authority. At St. Petersburg the *dvorniks* or house janitors were directed to spy upon the residents and to report their movements to the secret police. Executions, imprisonment, and exile multiplied until it seemed as if the government wished to terrify the terrorists.

Still the situation went from bad to worse. On December 1, 1879, as the imperial train was entering Moscow, it was wrecked by a mine. Alexander escaped because he had traveled in an earlier section. Three days later the "Executive Committee" issued a proclamation excusing the attempt and announcing that the czar had been condemned to death. On February 17, 1880, an explosion of dynamite in the guard room of the Winter Palace, just beneath the imperial dining-room, killed and maimed a large number of soldiers, but the imperial family escaped by a hair's breadth, as the czar had not entered the room. On the 24th of the same month Louis Melikof was placed in charge of the city of St. Petersburg, and eight days later there was an attempt upon his life. There was a panic in the capital, when a nihilist proclamation announced that these attempts would cease, provided the czar would renounce his autocracy and "leave the task of establishing social reforms to an assembly representing the entire Russian people."

R. Van Bergen

Whatever may have been his motive, Melikof urged the czar to try what conciliation would effect. Upon his advice, a large number of exiles in Siberia were pardoned, and persons imprisoned for political offenses were released. About 2,000 students expelled from the universities were readmitted, and in several cases the death sentence pronounced against nihilists was commuted. Only two men out of the sixteen convicted of the attempt to blow up the Winter Palace, were executed. The effect of this new policy was so satisfactory, that on the 18th of August, 1880, the czar revoked the ukase of February 24, and Melikof was appointed as Minister of the Interior. He advised the czar to grant a constitution, and in February 1881, placed before Alexander a plan to effect this important change gradually. It was discussed in the Council of State. The majority approved, but a bitter opposition was manifested by the other members. The czar himself was in favor of it, but the persons with whom he came into daily contact caused him to hesitate. He told Melikof that he would give his final decision on March 12.

On that day he had not made up his mind, but on the 13th, he ordered that Melikof's scheme should become a law, and that it be published in the Official Gazette. That afternoon, as he was returning from his usual drive, and his carriage was passing between the Catherine Canal and Michael's Garden, a bomb was thrown under his carriage and exploded, killing or wounding a number of the guard, but Alexander was unhurt. He was hurrying to assist the wounded, when another bomb exploded near him and he was dreadfully mangled. He regained consciousness for a moment while his attendants were bearing him to the palace, but died at 3.30 P.M., without having spoken a word.

A man named Rissakof, said to be a nihilist, was arrested for throwing the bomb; but there were ugly rumors that the assassination was committed under the direction of parties interested in maintaining an autocratic government at all risks. Owing to the secret proceedings in Russian courts, the murder of Alexander the Liberator still remains a mystery.

R. Van Bergen

XXVI

ALEXANDER III, THE PEASANTS' FRIEND

The atrocious death of The Liberator gave the throne to his son, who succeeded as Alexander III. The new czar was thirty-six years old. Nicholas, the eldest son of Alexander II, had died of consumption in 1865, and, since he had been the heir, his younger brother had not received any special training. His principal tutor had been Pobiedonostzeff, a man who believed in autocracy. He had imbued his pupil with a deeply religious feeling, and imparted to him a thorough knowledge of Russia's history. Alexander III was of powerful build and possessed unusual strength. He was loyal to his word, and tenacious in his likes and dislikes. Married to Princess Dagmar of Denmark, he was a model husband and father. His education made him a firm believer in autocracy.

The sudden and tragic death of his father moved him so deeply that he gave orders that the last wishes of the late czar should be respected. "Change nothing in my father's orders;" he said to Melikof; "they are his last will and testament." He issued two proclamations; in the first he announced that he would strengthen the bond with Poland and Finland, and thus gained the support of the Slavophils; and in the second, he reminded the peasants of the freedom given to them by his father, and ordered them to swear allegiance to himself and his heir. Six men and a woman implicated in the murder of the late czar were arrested, tried, condemned to death, and, with the exception of the woman, they were executed on April 15. The czar appointed his former tutor as Procurator of the Holy Synod. Pobiedonostzeff persuaded his pupil that this was not the time to make concessions. On the 11th of May, 1881, Alexander issued a proclamation in which he declared his intention to maintain the absolute power. Melikof resigned as Minister of the Interior and was replaced by Ignatieff, the former Russian Minister at Constantinople.

Shortly after his succession to the throne, Alexander made a journey to Moscow, and was everywhere received with unmistakable tokens of loyalty and affection. This confirmed his opinion that the great bulk of the population was satisfied with the form of government, and strengthened his determination to defend it.

In 1881, an anti-semitic movement was felt in Germany; that is, an outburst of hatred for the Jews broke out, which spread to Russia. It is not generally known that of all the Jews in the world, four fifths live in Russia in the southwest, in an area of 356,681 square miles. This is sometimes mentioned as the Jewish territory. Few of these people engage in agriculture; they are sometimes mechanics, but more often peddlers, storekeepers, bankers and moneylenders. The principal objection to them was that they succeed where others fail. In May, 1881, there were anti-Jewish riots at Kief and other places. Pobiedonostzeff's motto was, "One Russia, One Religion, One Czar;" prompted by him, Alexander did not take any energetic measures to suppress the disorder, for he, too, disliked to see in Russia a people differing in religion, language, and outward appearance. Ignatieff began a system of persecution by removing the Jews who had profited by the late czar's permission to settle anywhere, and when the act which recalled the Middle Ages was hotly condemned by the foreign press, even the Slavophils said that Ignatieff had gone too far. The persecution died out until 1884, when the Jews were deprived of their civil rights, and an attempt was made to compel them to enter the Greek Church. But the Jew is steadfast under persecution, and the only result was that some of them heartily joined the nihilists.

The public condemnation which followed these acts, induced Ignatieff to advise the czar to adopt Melikof's scheme of a constitution. Alexander did not understand this change of views and when de Giers was appointed Minister of Foreign Affairs, Ignatieff resigned. He was succeeded by D. Tolstoi.

Misunderstandings and the clashing of interests were dissolving the triple alliance of Russia, Austria, and Germany. This was apparent in the Balkan States which had been formed after the last Russo-Turkish war. Charles I, King of Roumania, was a German prince who mistrusted Russia's schemes. In March, 1882, Prince Milan Obrenovitch of Servia assumed the title of king, and the czar offered no objection. The ruler of Bulgaria was Alexander of Battenberg who was a relative of the czar and had served in the Russian army, which may have been the reason of his appointment. The Russian Minister at his court was evidently of the opinion that his word, as representative of the czar, was law, and when he found out that his orders were set at naught, he withdrew from his post, whereupon the Russian officers serving in the Bulgarian army, were dismissed. This gave grave offense at St. Petersburg, but the affair was arranged, and the Russian Minister returned. In September, 1885, there was a revolution in Sofia, the capital of Eastern Roumelia, when the crown was offered to Alexander of Battenberg, who accepted. He hastened to inform the czar, who was too angry to pay any attention to letters or telegrams.

Bulgaria and Eastern Roumelia, although united under one prince, sent deputations to St. Petersburg to appease the czar, but were informed that their future would be decided by the great powers. Soon after Servia declared war against Bulgaria; after a few unimportant skirmishes, they were driven back by Prince Alexander, who would have captured the capital Belgrad, if he had not been stopped by Austria's intervention. Alexander, after another fruitless attempt to mollify the czar, applied to the sultan, who appointed him as Governor-general over Eastern Roumelia for five years. The czar protested and invited the powers to a conference which was held at Constantinople on April 5, 1886. To the infinite disgust of the czar, the dispute was decided in favor of Prince Alexander.

Russia, however, had a pro-Russian party in Bulgaria. On August 21, 1886, Prince Alexander was kidnaped and carried across the Danube, after being compelled to abdicate. At Lemberg, in Austrian territory he was set free. The Bulgarians rallied under the President of the National Assembly and forced the pro-Russians to flee, after which Prince Alexander returned on the 3d of September. Once more he made an attempt to pacify the czar, but when his telegram remained unanswered, he abdicated three days later, rather than involve the country in a war with Russia. He left on the same day, to the sorrow of the people.

The czar was angry. He knew that Austria would not have dared oppose him unless assured of the support of Germany. The feeling in Russia grew more bitter when the election in Bulgaria showed a total defeat of the pro-Russian party, and the crown was offered to Prince Waldemar of Denmark, who declined at the instance of the czar. The Bulgarians then made an offer to Prince Ferdinand of Saxe-Coburg, who accepted, and in August made his formal entry in Tirnova. Alexander once more protested to the powers, but it passed unheeded and he urged the sultan to expel Ferdinand. Abdul Hamid declined with thanks, preferring to have as neighbor a small independent country to Russia. Alexander then demanded payment of the war indemnity due since the Treaty of San Stefano, but could obtain nothing except a profusion of excuses and apologies. Soon after the sultan had trouble in Armenia, which was Russia's latest resort to arouse public opinion against the Turk.

This is the age of colossal enterprises and combinations in every direction, in politics as well as in other branches of human activity. In Russia Slavophilism, gave way to Panslavism, that is, the scheme to unite all Slav nations. Germany was quick to respond with Pan Germanism, that is, to bring all German-speaking nations under one scepter. The czar, obeying this impulse, made every effort to convert the Baltic provinces,—which Germany called the German Provinces,—into Slavs by making the Russian language the only language that was taught in the schools; and Germany retaliated in the Polish provinces. Under these circumstances friendship ceased. Russia established a protective tariff, which was a rude blow to Germany's commerce; and that country replied by refusing to loan Russia any more money. The czar's government applied to France which responded with unexpected generosity. From that time Russia's internal improvements have been made with French capital.

Prudent as he was, Alexander allowed his anger and dislike to master him, when Prince Alexander of Battenberg was accepted as suitor to a daughter of Queen Victoria. Troops were hurried from the Caucasus into Poland, but Germany averted war by having the match broken off. When the present German emperor, William II, succeeded to the throne, he attempted to make friends with the czar by dismissing Prince Bismarck, in 1890, but Alexander could neither forgive nor forget. It was chiefly owing to this that

Russia and France drew closer together until it ended in an alliance.

Strong, self-willed, and masterful, Alexander did love his people in his own way. In January, 1884, he ordered the poll-tax to be abolished, and thereby relieved the peasants of a heavy burden; he also compelled the landowners to sell to their former serfs the land cultivated by them. Since the price was payable in installments and the owners needed the money, the government assumed the position of creditor, but Alexander reduced the total indebtedness by 12,000,000 rubles, and granted 5,000,000 rubles for the relief of overburdened villages. He calculated that the land would be paid for in 1930, when the title will be vested in the mir,— unless one of his successors should please to appropriate the past payments for other purposes.

In the black earth belt the allotments had been according to the needs of the population, but the increase among the people rendered them too small and several severe famines followed. The government tried to induce the surplus population to emigrate to Siberia, but the Russian peasant lacks education and has been held in tutelage so long that he is not fit for the life of a pioneer settler. Transportation facilities increased by the aid of French capital, and added to the prosperity of merchants and speculators, but did not help the moujik who did not know how to profit by them.

Alexander, as autocrat of all the Russias, did not suffer any authority but his own. The zemstvos, volosts, and mirs, were all placed under officials appointed by him. Every shadow of self-government was destroyed. This demanded a reorganization of the army, which was increased by 900,000 men. The reserves were called out once a year, and drilled as in actual war. Strategic railways were built for the speedy transportation of troops. Coast defenses were constructed and the navy was increased. In 1884, Batoum was closed as a port and converted into a naval base, and when England protested, claiming that this was in violation of the Treaty of Berlin,—as it was,—Russia, referring to the changes in the Balkan, inquired if the duty of observing the treaties was reserved exclusively for Russia.

Alexander's reign was especially discouraging for the Poles who still hoped for the revival of their country. Poles were made into Russians; but Panslavism demanded that the German should be banished. In 1887, Alexander ordered that, when a foreign landowner in Poland died, his estate must be sold unless his heirs had been residents of Poland before this order was published. Germany, suffering from Pan-Germanism, collected several thousand Russian Poles who had settled in Germany, and put them across the frontier. Russia replied by making a law in the Baltic provinces that nothing but Russian could be taught in any school, and that no more Lutheran churches could be built without the permission of the Holy Synod.

Then came Finland's turn. In 1890, Russian money, Russian stamps, and worse than that, Russian taxes were introduced. There were loud protests, which received courteous answers, but the process continued. In 1891, the Finnish Committee at St. Petersburg, which had directed the affairs of Finland, was abolished, and Russian censorship abolished the free press. The Russian language was made obligatory, and the Finns who could afford it emigrated to the United States and settled in the northwest.

In 1890, Alexander ordered the construction of the Trans-Siberian railway, of which more will be said in the chapter on Asiatic Russia.

All these years Alexander had battled with nihilism and

revolution. His policy neither gave nor asked for quarter. In May, 1888, an army officer named Timovief made an attempt upon the czar's life. On October 29th of the same year, as he was traveling in southern Russia an accident occurred in which twenty-one were killed and many injured; it was ascribed to nihilists, but may have been caused by defects. Be that as it may, Alexander never recovered from the shock. In March, 1890, another plot against his life was discovered. In November, 1891, the secret police came on the scent of a conspiracy at Moscow, and in April, 1894, they learned of one at St. Petersburg. In constant fear of assassination, Alexander resided at Gatschina, twenty-five miles south of St. Petersburg, as in an armed fortress. The never-ceasing tension wore out the strong man. He caught cold and suffering from inflammation of the kidneys he went south, but experienced no relief. He died on the 1st of November, 1894.

In his private life he was essentially a good man; as czar, he acted according to his convictions. He gave much thought to the welfare of the peasants and as such deserved the surname of The Peasants' Friend.

XXVII

RUSSIA UNDER THE PRESENT CZAR NICHOLAS II

"Neglect nothing that can make my son truly a man!" This was the instruction given by Alexander to the tutors of his son. Consequently, Nicholas in his youth was allowed to indulge in manly exercises and sports, while special tutors taught him mathematics, natural philosophy, history, political economy, English, French, and German, besides his native language. Destined for the throne, he began his military career at the age of thirteen as hetman of the Cossacks, and passed successively through the different grades. In 1889, at the age of twenty-one, he was appointed president of a committee to prepare plans for the Trans-Siberian railway, and the following year he made a tour in the Far East, visiting China and Japan. In the last-named country he was attacked and wounded by a police officer who had been brooding over the wrongs which his country had suffered at the hands of Russia. Nicholas recovered and proceeded to Vladivostok, where he initiated the building of the great continental line. He returned to St. Petersburg by way of Siberia and Moscow, and was the first czar who had ever visited his Asiatic empire.

Born on May 18, 1868, he was twenty-six years old when he

was called to the throne. He announced that he would "promote the progress and peaceful glory of our beloved Russia, and the happiness of all our faithful subjects." On the 26th of November, 1894, the czar married Princess Alice of Hesse-Darmstadt, the granddaughter of Queen Victoria, who, on entering the Greek Church, received the name of Alexandra Feodorofna. The czar retained his father's ministers, except that Prince Khilkof, who had learned practical railroading in the United States, was appointed Minister of Public Works. Pobiedonostzeff continued as Procurator of the Holy Synod.

Nicholas showed greater leniency toward Poland and Finland than his father had done. He revoked several of his father's ukases and seemed to be willing to treat them fairly. Finland's forests are a source of great prosperity and the Russian officials have long been anxious to secure a share. When the Secretary of State for Finland resigned, General Kuropatkin became Minister of War, and he wished to introduce Russia's military system. General Bobrikof, a brusque and haughty man, was appointed Governor-general with instructions to proceed with the conversion of the Finns into Slavs. He convoked an extraordinary session of the Diet, January 24, 1899, and submitted Kuropatkin's scheme, with a strong hint that it must pass. The Diet ignored the hint and rejected the scheme, whereupon Bobrikof ignored the Diet and published it as a law to go into effect in 1903. An imperial ukase of February 15, 1899, reorganized the Diet according to a plan drawn up by Pobiedonostzeff. Bobrikof increased the rigor of the press censorship, but the Finns remained within the law. A petition was circulated which in ten days secured 500,000 signatures, and a delegation was sent to St. Petersburg to present it. The delegation was not admitted.

In January, 1895, the czar received a deputation of all classes

R. Van Bergen

of his subjects who hinted that the zemstvos might be used as the germ of a constitutional government. He replied that he believed in autocracy and that he intended to maintain it as his predecessors had done. On the 26th of May, 1896, he was crowned at Moscow with more than usual splendor, and in the same year he and the czarina made a tour through Europe. After visiting the German Emperor and Queen Victoria, they went to Paris where the czar, after reviewing 100,000 soldiers declared that the Empire and the Republic were united in indissoluble friendship. The visit was returned by the President of the French Republic, M. Faure, in August, 1897. On this occasion the world received notice that an alliance existed between the two powers, and that, if one of them was attacked by more than one power, the other would assist with the whole of its military and naval strength, and peace could be concluded only in concert between the allies.

Two great reforms are noticeable under the present reign. The sale of spirits has greatly decreased since the government took the monopoly of the manufacture and sale of liquor. The French loans made the establishment of the gold standard possible and speculation in Russian paper money ceased.

The completion of the Trans-Siberian Railway aroused great expectation for the future of Russia's commerce. The war with Japan has prevented the possibility of estimating the effect it will have upon oceanic trade. But Russia's manufactures have had a wonderful increase; its effect is shown in the population of the cities. In 1870, Russia contained only six cities with a population of over 100,000; their number was doubled in 1897. Warsaw, the old capital of Poland, had 243,000 inhabitants in 1865; in 1897, they had increased to 615,000. Lotz, also in Poland, rose from 12,000 to 315,000. This cannot fail to exert a powerful influence upon the future of the empire; first, on account of the creation of a middle class which, even at this early day, numbers nine per cent of the population; and next, because the mechanics and factory hands are recruited from among the peasants, who thus are brought into daily contact with more intelligent people, and acquire new ideas and new necessities. The official class is bitterly opposed to this new departure, because it foreshadows the day when the drag upon Russia will be cast off.

Nicholas seems to have reversed his father's policy in the Balkan States. He also acted in concert with Europe in 1896, when trouble arose between Turkey and Greece. It began in Crete, where Turk and Christian could not agree. Stories of massacres infuriated the Greeks and the king had to choose between a revolution and a declaration of war. In April, 1897, an army of 80,000 men under Prince George crossed into Thessaly, but was driven back by a Turkish army of 150,000 men. Prince George had invaded Crete in February, but the powers compelled him to evacuate the island. The czar interceded with the sultan, and the absurd war was ended.

The Slavophils, after their failure in the Balkan provinces had excited the Armenians in the provinces near the Russian Caucasus. They attacked the Kurds, a nomadic tribe of Mussulmans, when the Turks took the side of their co-religionists and treated the Armenians with no soft hand. The Panslavists demanded autonomy for Armenia, but this did not suit Prince Lobanof, who had succeeded de Giers as Minister of Foreign Affairs, because he feared trouble in the Caucasus. In 1895, Russia, France, and England, presented a note to the sultan, suggesting the appointment of a high commissioner, the abolition of torture, and reforms in taxation. Turkey agreed, but Shakir Pasha, the high commissioner, failed to restore order and the disorder threatened to become a revolt. Even in Constantinople a condition of anarchy prevailed.

The atrocities committed by the Turks aroused indignation everywhere, when the Armenians seized the Ottoman Bank, but the conspirators were forced to flee from the building and to seek refuge on an English yacht. The Turks were furious and killed more than 5,000 Armenians. Again the powers remonstrated; but at this time it began to dawn upon the public that the Armenians were a least quite as much to blame as the Turks, and the interest subsided. Russia had discovered that the Armenians are undesirable citizens, and sent back some 40,000 of them who had settled in the Russian Caucasus. Germany, intent upon securing concessions from Turkey, left the sultan a free hand; meanwhile the British public was engrossed by the Boer war, and the Armenians, seeing that they were left to their own devices, subsided.

The civilized world was startled when, on August 24, 1898, Russia issued a note to the powers, declaring that "military and naval budgets attack public prosperity at its very source, and divert national energies from useful aims," and suggesting a conference to discuss the subject of displacing war by an International Court.

The note received generous applause, especially in the United States and Great Britain, the two foremost nations devoted to the arts of peace. The several governments agreed to participate in the proposed conference. The place selected was The Hague, the capital of the Netherlands, where the sessions opened on May 18, 1899.

Of all the great powers, the United States was the only one unreservedly in favor of an arrangement whereby war would be prevented. Most of the other powers looked upon an International Court as visionary, and so far as the ostensible purpose is concerned, the conference was a failure. Still, it bore fruit in defining and adding strength to international law. Among its most important results is the clause that "When a conflict seems imminent, one or several powers shall have the right to offer mediation, and its exercise shall not be regarded as an unfriendly act." A permanent Court of Arbitration was established at The Hague. It is composed of judges selected from a list on which every country is represented. On the 29th of July, the delegates of sixteen nations signed the protocol embodying the conclusions; it was afterwards signed by sixteen more. It remained, however, with the United States, to give vitality to an institution which was looked upon with ill favor by many governments.

Although the reign of terror from the nihilists has passed, political murder is still rampant in Russia, and recent events in the Far East have caused a renewal of the agitation for reforms. In 1904, the Governor-general of Finland was assassinated, and soon afterwards, the hated and dreaded Minister of the Interior de Plehve shared that fate. His successor seems to be anxious to grant greater liberties to the people. The united action of the zemstvos, and the final issue of the war in the Far East, may have important results. Nicholas II, amid all his perplexities, was made glad by the birth of a son and heir, who received the name of Alexis.

R. Van Bergen

XXVIII

THE ORIGIN AND GROWTH OF
THE ASIATIC EMPIRE

A close study of the history of Asiatic Russia reveals the fact that, until within a comparatively recent date, the Russian government had no fixed policy in or toward Asia. There was a national instinct which impelled Russia eastward. Twice had Europe been invaded by Asiatic hordes, and, owing to its position, Russia was doomed to bear the brunt of the onset. Russia's history points out a ceaseless desire to be a European nation, to share with Europe its progress and its burdens. It is within a few years that the heir to the throne first visited the extensive Asiatic dominions. No czar had ever put foot in them. Until the reign of Nicholas I (1825-1855), the Russian Empire spread eastward much as the United States expanded westward, by individual effort.

The movement began in 1558, when Ivan the Terrible granted to Gregory Strogonof ninety-two miles of waste land on the banks of the Kama. The new owner explored the mineral resources of the Urals, crossed the mountains, and found himself in the kingdom of Sibir. Strogonof had become acquainted with one Yermak or Irmak, a Cossack and captain of a robber band known as the Good Companions of the Don. He had been condemned to death, if the government could lay hands on him, which, on account of the sparsity of the population, was exceedingly doubtful. Strogonof discussed with him a raid into Sibir, and the Cossack consented, provided his pardon could be secured. Strogonof went to Moscow and submitted his scheme to Ivan who gave his approval. Upon his return to the Urals, Strogonof found that he had 850 men, Russians, Cossacks, Tartars, and German and Polish prisoners of war, all hardy adventurers. They marched east terrifying the natives with their firelocks, and levying tribute, that is, taking whatever was worth the trouble. They defeated the khan, and took his capital, Sibir, on the Irtish. Yermak then visited Moscow, where he was the hero of the day. Had he not struck at the very heart of the mysterious continent whence so much trouble and disgrace had come upon Russia? And had he not exacted tribute from the very people who not very long ago held Russia under tribute.

Yermak was therefore praised and entertained and graciously told to go ahead, Ivan had neither men nor money to spare, but he was quite willing that these adventurers should despoil the Asiatics, instead of holding up Russian travelers and traders. Ivan gave him a suit of armor as a token of good will. After Yermak's return to Siberia, he was surprised by the natives and drowned by the weight of his armor as he was trying to escape by swimming the Irtish. (1584.) Other Cossacks had heard of his success and followed his example. In 1587, Tobolsk was founded on the Irtish, ten miles below Sibir.

There was little or no communication between Siberia and Moscow, owing to the distance separating them, and the successors of Ivan had ample trouble on their hands. It was, therefore, left to the Cossacks to make such explorations and conquests as they could. In 1619, Tomsk was founded. Farther and farther did the Cossacks advance among the isolated tribes. In 1632, a log fort was built where Yakoutsk now stands, and six years later they gazed upon the broad waters of the Pacific and planted the czar's flag on the shore of the Sea of Okhotsk.

It was a congenial occupation for the Cossack, to roam where he pleased and to take what suited his fancy, and he did not lack either the skill or the courage needed by the explorer. In 1639, a party of Cossacks under Max Perfirief, discovered the Upper Amoor, and heard tales of such vast wealth that they hastened to Yakoutsk and placed their discovery before Peter Petrovitch, the first Russian Governor.

Men and money were scarce, but the governor, after many efforts managed to collect 132 men whom he placed in command of Vassili Poyarkof, with instructions to do the best he could. The party started on the 15th of July, 1643, and followed the usual course with the natives with the result that he returned to Yakoutsk in June 1646, having lost most of his men in attacks by infuriated and outraged natives, but in possession of a fund of information, and some skins as tribute.

During the reign of Alexis Michaelovitch (1645-1676), explorations of the Amoor regions were pursued vigorously. A young officer of considerable wealth, named Khabarof, offered to conduct an expedition at his own expense. This was gladly accepted, and he left Yakoutsk in 1649. He reached the Amoor and formed a line of forts, and met a small party among whom was the khan, who asked what his object was. Khabarof replied that he had come to trade, but that the czar would probably take the khan under his powerful protection in return for a small annual tribute. The khan did not answer, and Khabarof after burning most of the forts and leaving some of his men in another, returned to

Yakoutsk to report.

In June, 1651, he was on the way back to the Amoor, where he came in conflict with the Manchus. He, however, forced his way, and gained for the Russians the reputation that they were "devils, who would make gridirons of the parents to roast the children on." At this time a report that the Amoor region contained untold wealth reached Moscow, where it produced an effect very similar to that felt in Spain after the return of Columbus.

Alexis intended to send an expedition of 3,000 men to occupy and hold this treasure grove, but he was prudent enough to dispatch an officer to order Khabarof to Moscow, so that he might learn the facts. This officer, Simovief left Moscow in March, 1652, and met Khabarof in August of the following year. Leaving the command to his lieutenant Stepanof, Khabarof obeyed the czar's call. He arrived at Moscow and after the czar had heard his report, the expedition was given up, but Alexis wrote to Stepanof, upon whom he conferred some honors, and told him to continue the good work.

The interest manifested by the czar inaugurated an exploration fever among the Russian authorities. Pashkof, the Governor of Yeniseisk started on the 18th of July, 1656, for the Amoor at the head of 400 Cossacks; in 1658, he built a fort which was the beginning of Nerchinsk. It was 1662 before he returned to Yeniseisk.

Unfortunately the Russians came into a clash with the Manchus, at that time in full vigor; they had made themselves masters of China, and their emperor, Kang-hi, was an exceptionably able and strong man. He did not want war, but on the other hand he did not intend to suffer an injustice.

When the government at Moscow became aware that further encroachment would entail a war with China an ambassador, Feodor Golovin, was dispatched to come to an understanding. He left Moscow on January 20, 1686, but took his time. Kang-hi had been notified, and ambassadors were sent from Peking to meet Golovin. The Russian met the Chinese at Nerchinsk on the 22d August, 1689, and on the 27th the terms of a treaty were agreed upon. Two days later the treaty was exchanged. Russia was compelled to withdraw from the Amoor. After this no changes in the boundary line occurred until after the year 1847.

In 1707, Kamtschatka was annexed to Russia, and two years later the first prisoners were sent to Siberia. They were prisoners of war and natives of conquered European provinces who objected to Muscovite rule. About 14,000 persons were sent the first year, but many died from the hardships suffered on the road.

Besides Siberia, Russia in Asia consists of:

I. The Caucasus. It was Peter the Great who, in 1722, invaded Dagestan and seized the greater part of this territory. We have seen how the mountaineers defended their liberty under Schamyl,[11] and it was left to his son Alexander to annex it and make it part of the Russian Empire. Including Trans Caucasia, it covers an area of 180,843 square miles,— or about that of Colorado and Utah, and contains a population of 8,350,000.

[Footnote 11: See p. 209]

II. The Kirghiz Steppe. This is a country of plains, unfit for agriculture and still inhabited by nomads who live in tents and wander with their flocks over the 755,793 square miles of territory. They are divided into three hordes or families, one of which surrendered to Anne Ivanovna in 1734. In 1869 the Kirghiz, together with the Cossacks of the Don, revolted, but in the autumn of 1870, order was restored. For administrative purposes, it is divided into:

III. Transcaspia, which, as the name indicates, includes the region east of the Caspian Sea. It contains an area of 383,618 square miles with a population estimated at 352,000. Like the Kirghiz Steppe, it is unfit for agriculture, although it contains several oases. It was formed into a province by Alexander III. in 1881.

IV. Turkestan contains 409,414 square miles with a population of 3,341,000. The valleys of the Oxus and Jaxartes are very fertile, but the rest of the extensive province is almost a desert. The Oxus or Amu Daria once formed the boundary of the empires of Cyrus and Alexander. It was conquered step by step, and after many struggles with the Turkomans and Kirghiz to whom it originally belonged.

V. The Khanates, so called because they once formed the territory of the Khans of Khiva and Bokhara. This province embraces 114,320 square miles with a population of 3,200,000. Both are recent acquisitions. It was the war with Khiva, in 1872, which first drew the attention of Europe to Russia's expansion in Central Asia. There had been some doubts as to the wisdom of permitting Russia to add more territory to her already enormous domain, but they had been allayed by a circular note to the powers, issued by Prince Gortchakof, the Minister of Foreign Affairs, on November 21, 1864. He declared that Russia had been brought into contact with a number of half-savage tribes who proved a constant menace to the security of the Empire, and that the only means of maintaining order on the frontier, was to bring them under submission. This, he said, had been done by the United States, and was nothing but a measure necessary for self-defense.

This reasoning was self-evident, but in 1873 the press of Great Britain asked when and where this necessity would cease. Count Schouvalof was sent to London and in several interviews with Lord Granville, he stated distinctly and plainly that Russia had no intention to annex any more territory in Central Asia. He declared[12] solemnly with regard to Khiva that "not only was it far from the intention of the emperor to take possession of Khiva, but positive orders had been prepared to prevent it, and directions given that the conditions imposed should be such as would not in any way lead to the prolonged occupation of Khiva."

[Footnote 12: Parliamentary Papers, Central Asia. 1873.]

Notwithstanding this positive declaration, Khiva was annexed on the 10th of June, 1873. Four months afterwards, on the 10th of October, a treaty was signed by the Khan of Bokhara, giving to Russia free navigation on the Oxus, and other privileges. It has never been formally annexed, but is to all intents and purposes Russian territory.

XXIX

RUSSIAN METHODS. THE WAR WITH JAPAN

At the time when the United States and the commercial powers of Europe were discussing the opening of Japan, Russia resolved, if possible, to forestall them. In 1847, the czar appointed a young general, Nicholas Muravieff, as governor of Eastern Siberia. Shortly after entering upon his office he sent an officer named Vagarof, who had explored the Amoor River, back to it with four Cossacks to make an extensive report. The party left Strelka in the spring of 1848, but was never heard of again. Suspecting that they had been captured by the Chinese, a demand was made for their surrender on the plea that they were deserters, but the Chinese replied that they knew nothing of them. Meanwhile Muravieff had ordered the exploration of the shore of the Sea of Okhotsk and the mouth of the Amoor. These orders were promptly executed, and in 1850 Lieutenant Orloff entered the river from the sea. The following year Captain Nevilskoi, who had come out in the *Baikal*, sent a boat up the river and laid the foundations of Nikolayefsk and Mariinsk, thereby securing a foothold on the Lower Amoor, knowing all the time that this was Chinese territory, and that Russia was at peace with China. The survey of the Sea of Okhotsk was not neglected. Port Imperial on the coast of Manchuria was discovered and occupied, and Urup, one of the Kurile

Islands, was seized. When Commodore Perry arrived off the coast of Japan, he was watched by Admiral Poutiatine in command of the *Pallas*, *Vostok*, *Olivutzu* and *Menzikoff*. Aniwa Bay was seized the same year, and Russians landed on the west coast of what is known as Saghalien, but was known and owned by the Japanese under the name of Karafuto.

The Crimean War gave Muravieff a pretext to violate farther the treaty with China. He claimed that the settlements on the Pacific, as well as the Russian ships, were in need of supplies, and that the ocean route was closed by the allied fleets. Was it Muravieff's duty to furnish those supplies? In that case, any reference to the ocean route was preposterous, because it is absurd to suppose that supplies would be sent from Eastern Siberia to the north Pacific coast by such a route; and if he had furnished them before by the overland route through Siberia, why, that road was open to him. What he needed was a pretext to secure the occupation of Japan, or at least of some of its islands, before the other powers could know of it; and for that purpose, it was necessary to be in possession of the lower Amoor. Perry's energetic action thwarted him; but he could not know that. What he did know was that China was not in a condition to oppose him, and that the other powers need not know what he was doing.

He determined to send an expedition strong enough to insure respect, and lost no time in preparing it. Fifty barges, a steamer, and numerous rafts, a thousand Cossacks with cannon, the whole commanded by Muravieff himself, left Shilkinsk on the 24th of May, 1854. Following the usual custom, the expedition was accompanied by scientific men to survey the river, prepare maps, explore the country, and examine its resources. At ten A.M., June 8, they arrived at Aigun where Muravieff was received by the Chinese authorities, who displayed about the same number of armed men, but such men and such arms! Firelocks dating from the time of Kang-hi—1689,—convinced Muravieff that fifty Cossacks could put these braves to rout. Not caring to arouse Chinese hostility for fear that his schemes might attract attention, Muravieff did not resent it when the Chinese forbade him to enter the town; he continued on his journey, and on the 27th of June arrived at Mariinsk. After sending part of his force to Nikolayefsk, he went on to Port Imperial where he met Admiral Poutiatine. They discussed the situation, and Poutiatine left for Japan on the *Diana*.

Muravieff hurried back as he had come, and prepared another expedition which he took down the river in 1855. In that year he sent three thousand Cossacks, and five hundred colonists down the Amoor, together with horses, cattle, provisions, and military stores. This activity could not escape the Chinese who dispatched four officials to Nikolayefsk to protest against the invasion of their territory. They arrived in July, and were entertained by Muravieff with a review of his forces; after this hint he simply dismissed them. At this time the settlements which stood in such urgent need of supplies, were Mariinsk, which consisted of two log cabins, Nikolayefsk numbered ten, and Castries Bay had "four badly built huts."[13]

[Footnote 13: Ravenstein, Russians on the Amoor.]

In a remarkably short time we hear of the indefatigable Muravieff at St. Petersburg urging the annexation of the Amoor. He was opposed by the czar's ministers, but succeeded in convincing the emperor that China could offer no resistance, and that the powers need not hear of it until it was too late. Thus he secured large supplies of men and money. In the beginning of 1857, he was back at his post, and on the 1st of June he dispatched Colonel Ushakof with six hundred men from Shilkinsk, and soon after followed him with a brigade of Cossack infantry and a regiment of cavalry, to garrison the forts which he constructed at strategic points.

Seizing the opportunity of China's distress caused by the war with England and France, Muravieff demanded the cession of the Amoor Valley. The Chinese were helpless. On the 28th of May, 1858, a treaty was signed at Aigun, giving to Russia the left bank of the Amoor down to the Ussuri, and both banks below that confluent, besides the right to navigate the Sungari and Ussuri rivers. Russia gave absolutely nothing in return. Meanwhile Count Poutiatine had been sent from St. Petersburg to watch the allies and to profit by any blunder which they or the Chinese might make. Poutiatine stopped in Japan, claiming that the Koreans had given him the privilege of establishing a coaling station at Port Hamilton, but knowing that Great Britain would certainly investigate his claim, he did not press it. He tried to seize the Japanese Island Tsushima in the southern entrance to the Japan Sea, and midway between Japan and Korea; but a polite and firm invitation from the British admiral to leave that island, and the admiral's insistence to remain until after he had left it, spoiled that little game. Poutiatine then proceeded to China where he proposed to help put down the Tai P'ing rebellion in return for the cession of Manchuria to Russia. This handsome offer was politely declined. Once again Muravieff hurried to St. Petersburg; upon his advice the newly acquired territory was officially annexed, and, by ukase of October 31, joined to the littoral of the Sea of Okhotsk and Kamtschatka under the name of Maritime Province of Eastern Siberia, with Nikolayevsk as capital. Muravieff remained in supreme command.

The tireless empire builder was again on the Pacific Coast in 1858. On May 21, he founded Blagovestchensk and, after descending the river, laid the foundation of Khabarofka, at the mouth of the Ussuri. In October he was back at Kiakhta, arranging for the postal service between St. Petersburg and the extreme east. On the 26th of August, he was created Count Amoorsky, or Count of the Amoor, a promotion which he had well earned. On the 31st of December, a remarkable ukase was published, beginning "Now that Russia has regained possession of this valuable region, etc." The entire territory of Eastern Siberia contained 740,922 square miles, a territory equal to that of all the Atlantic Coast States, together with Indiana, Ohio, West Virginia, Kentucky, Tennessee, Alabama, and Mississippi. This did not include the Amoor Province, which was placed under the administration of a governor and eighteen officials, who received a combined annual salary of $18,873.60, of which the governor received $4680.

Muravieff was back at his post in 1859. Both he and Poutiatine tried to induce the Japanese to give up Karafuto (Saghalien), but without success. At this time there was again trouble between China and the allied British and French, and when in 1860, a British-French force marched on Peking, Russia had sent another empire builder, General Ignatieff, to watch if he could not secure something. He did; when the allies entered Peking, Ignatieff sought Prince Kung and told him that the "foreign devils" would surely seize the country unless some strong power compelled them to leave. Russia was willing to do this, because she had always been fond of China; and all she asked was a strip of outlying territory of no value to China. Prince Kung gladly signed away the whole east coast of Manchuria, six hundred miles long; and Ignatieff redeemed his promise by visiting Lord Elgin and Baron Gros, the British and French plenipotentiaries. After paying them some flattering compliments, he made the remark that the Peiho river would freeze in a few days, and if they did not get out at once, they would have to stay all winter in Peking. The two gentlemen finished their business in a hurry, packed up, and left, but not without thanking Ignatieff for his kindness and reporting the matter to their government, which did not hear of the Russian's diplomacy until a year later. This is how Russia extended her empire on the Pacific Coast.

For many years the efforts to secure the whole island of Karafuto continued and Japan saw that war must follow unless a sacrifice was made. In 1875, Japan surrendered the island, in return for the Kurile group, but the Japanese treasured in their hearts the loss and disgrace. It was this which caused the assault upon the present czar, when he was traveling in Japan.

In 1894 the war between Japan and China broke out, and when China, humbled, sued for peace, Japan demanded the cession of the Liaotung Peninsula,—where Port Arthur is located,—besides making other conditions. When this became known, Russia, after securing the help of Germany and France, gave Japan the "friendly advice," which was really a threat, not to take that peninsula. Japan, single-handed, could not fight the three powers, and gave way; but every Japanese, high or low, young or old, was determined to pay off Russia. They bought or built war vessels everywhere and increased their army. Russia did not like this, and proposed that Japan should take all the islands in the Pacific, the Philippines, Hawaii, Borneo, etc., and leave the continent of Asia to Russia. Japan declined, and went on building ships. In the end of 1898, Russia announced that she had "leased" the very Liaotung Peninsula which she had prevented Japan from taking. Japan understood, as the whole world did, that this "lease" meant possession. The Japanese statesmen did not protest, because there was but one protest that Russia would heed,—an appeal to arms. That was Japan's method when, in 1899, Alexander Pavloff, the Russian minister in Korea, secured from that government a concession in the port of Masampo, opening into the entrance to the Japan Sea. Japan's demand was: Let Masampo go, or it means war. And Russia evacuated Masampo, while Pavloff was told that he might take a furlough. Then came 1900, the Boxer troubles and the international march upon Peking. Japanese officers took note of the Russian troops, leaving the Russians to do the same with their soldiers. Japan never ceased her preparations. In the latter part of 1901, Marquis Ito Hirobumi visited the United States and crossed over to England, where he proposed an offensive-defensive alliance. British statesmen hesitated, when Ito told them in plain terms that if no such treaty was concluded, he was authorized to go on to Russia, and make the best terms he could for his country.

Meanwhile Pavloff had returned to Seoul, the capital of Korea, and by means best known to Russian diplomats, was trying to gain a foothold on the Peninsula. Under the pretext of a timber concession, the Russians constructed a fort on the Korean side of the Yalu river,—where it was afterwards discovered by newspaper correspondents. Russia had secured control of Manchuria with its 362,310 square miles and 11,250,000 population, and none of the powers dared protest. Japan was ready. Could she allow the "peaceful" absorption of Korea, as that of Manchuria had been accomplished? Safe in the offensive-defensive alliance with Great Britain, Japan approached Russia in a dignified manner, to be put off with vague replies. After six months of patience, Japan broke off diplomatic intercourse, and, as this is considered equal to a declaration of war, she struck and hit hard.

XXX

RUSSIA LOSES HER PRESTIGE

When, in February, 1904, the world was startled by the Japanese guns in the harbor of Chemulpo (Korea), one of Russia's well-known diplomats, speaking in defense of his country, said: "Ours has been a peaceful absorption." Another statesman, pleading for sympathy, remarked pathetically: "We were unprepared for war." The two advocates of Russia's cause spoke the truth, but they did not proclaim the whole truth.

Ever since Muravieff Amoorsky began the peaceful absorption of Manchuria by seizing the coastline of that province, Russia has extended her dominions using no other weapon than her prestige, that is, the dread inspired by her name, power, and resources. Repeated protests from Great Britain remained unheeded, because the czar's government was convinced that they would not be emphasized by a resort to arms. The semi-civilized tribes of Central Asia were unable, of course, to oppose the Russian advance; and China was justly afraid of defying the great northern power. Thus the peaceful absorption continued with such ease that the Russian tchinovnik ended in believing in their country's prestige. Herein lies the principal cause of the astounding history of the war with Japan.

Although Russia repeatedly agreed to evacuate Manchuria, her actions in the construction of railways and other roads, the opening of mines, the enormous capital expended in creating a commercial emporium in Dalny, and her jealousy in excluding foreigners from that territory,—all this was ample evidence that nothing short of compulsion would cause her to withdraw. Besides, Alexander Pavloff, the Russian Minister in Korea, was anxious to emulate Count Cassini, his former chief at Peking. He was constantly plotting to secure a foothold in the Peninsula. In 1903, it was announced that a Russian company had obtained a timber concession on the Yalu River. A few months afterwards, some American newspaper correspondents with the Japanese army discovered the ruins of a Russian fort on that river, securely screened from indiscreet eyes, but in a fine position to control the passage. That was the timber concession.

Russia's policy, therefore, was a serious menace to Japan. But Japan did not purpose to draw ridicule by unavailing protests. Feverishly the preparations for more emphatic action were continued; in the latter part of 1903, Japan was ready. Safe from a possible European intervention by her treaty with Great Britain, Japan reminded Russia of her promise to evacuate Manchuria on October 7, and requested an explanation for not keeping the pledge. Russia, with a blind faith in her prestige, replied that the affair did not concern Japan but China, whereupon Japan made a proposition concerning Manchuria and Korea which would be acceptable. With studied contempt replies from the czar were held back beyond the time permitted by international courtesy. Moreover their tenor was not only unsatisfactory, but was also calculated to exasperate the proud Japanese. When the final preparations were made, Japan instructed her minister to St. Petersburg, to demand his passports,—an act equivalent to a declaration of war.

R. Van Bergen

The tchinovnik doubted their senses. Russia maintained that a severance of diplomatic relations did not necessarily imply an appeal to the sword, when the news flashed over the wires that the Russian war vessels Varyag and Koreyetz had been blown up at Chemulpo to escape being captured. The world was still marveling at Japan's audacity when it was informed that three other Russian war vessels had been disabled owing to a night torpedo attack under Admiral Togo.

Why was the Russian fleet, numerically superior to that of Japan, divided? The answer is found in that fatal word: prestige. Pavloff in Korea had requested the presence of the two doomed ships, to keep the Japanese in awe. Admiral Stark lay under the guns of impregnable Port Arthur, trusting to the prestige, when the illusion vanished. There was still the Vladivostok squadron; it made an effort to induce Togo to leave Port Arthur by making a raid upon the north coast of Japan, but in vain. Beyond sinking a few unarmed merchantmen, nothing of importance was accomplished.

The czar's choice to restore Russia's naval prestige, fell upon Admiral Makaroff. At about the same time, General Kuropatkin, the former Minister of War, was charged with punishing Japan for her insolence. His departure for the Far East was theatrical. After many genuflexions before sacred eikons, he promised to restore Russia's prestige by dictating terms of peace in Tokyo.

Makaroff was less enthusiastic, and perhaps more in earnest. It is asserted that he restored discipline in a sadly demoralized fleet. He was enticed out of Port Arthur's shelter by a small fleet of the enemy's cruisers sent out as a decoy. When he discovered Togo's ironclads he returned to port, but his flagship struck a mine at the entrance to Port Arthur and sunk. The Admiral, as well as his guest, the noted battle painter Verestchagin, perished.

With Togo blockading Port Arthur and Admiral Kaminura guarding Vladivostok, the Japanese secured the freedom of the sea, and began to pour troops into Korea. This was greeted with acclamation by the tchinovnik who, after their naval misfortunes, claimed that the situation would soon be reversed by the army. Some Japanese soldiers were landed openly at Chemulpo, but the bulk went ashore in a well-concealed harbor south of the Yalu River. General Kuroki was in command.

Meanwhile Kuropatkin was in Manchuria busy organizing the army when not obstructed by Viceroy Alexieff. Such troops as he found were capable of rendering good service in hunting down Chinese brigands, but, as the sequel proved, the army had also been nurtured upon that most indigestible material, prestige. To the wonder of Europe,—and to a less degree of America,—Kuroki crossed the Yalu and sent the czar's dreaded soldiers flying before him. (May 1, 1904.)

Once more, and for the last time, did the Russian fleet at Port Arthur attempt a sortie. It failed, and its fate was sealed.

While the wreckage of Russia's once proud fleet lay concealed in Port Arthur's inner basin, the Japanese, after scouring the waters to clear them from mines, landed troops on the Liaotung Peninsula, claimed by Japan after the war with China, but despoiled of it by Russia's peaceful absorption. In 1894, Port Arthur was taken in a day from the Chinese: the Russians defended the impregnable fortress for six months. "Our prestige demands that the enemy shall not capture Port Arthur," cried the tchinovnik, and Kuropatkin was ordered to General Stoessel's rescue. The attempt failed, and General Nogi could pursue the siege without being disturbed. (June 14-15, 1904.)

A stolid, ignorant, and densely superstitious people was at

war with a rejuvenated nation keenly alive to the power of education. That is the secret. Man for man, Russia would have won. But the resourcefulness of the little brown man more than offset the Russian's physical superiority. As the year 1905 dawned, the fall of Port Arthur was made known to the world.

Slowly, but heralded by the marvels it would accomplish, the Baltic fleet under Rojestvensky sailed to Madagascar, welcome to whatever aid the French ally could bestow. Japan said nothing, but made a note of it. She cleaned and scraped her sea-worn, battle-scarred vessels, under the supervision of grim, silent Togo. Oyama, the Japanese commander-in-chief, reenforced by the veterans of Kuroki and Nogi, was playing with Kuropatkin until he had the game in his hand. After ten days of hard fighting, the discomfited Russians made a masterly retreat to the Sha river, after evacuating Mukden, the cradle of the present Chinese dynasty, (August 26-September 4, 1904.)

Kuropatkin deserved credit for the manner in which he extricated the remains of the czar's army. Oyama did not feel safe in following up the pursuit. His game was that of a skillful chess player. First make sure of the result with mathematical precision, then strike. The Japanese were deaf to the demand for brilliant dashes.

After the battle of Liao-yang, the armies seemed idle so far as news from the front went. Oyama attacked his former antagonist on the Shakhe River and drove the discomfited Russians beyond Tie pass. General Kuropatkin was superseded by his former subordinate Linievitch who, however, accomplished nothing to warrant his promotion.

Meanwhile the Baltic fleet left the hospitable shores of Madagascar, proclaiming its search for Togo, together with the determination to punish the impertinent Japanese. In the latter part of May, 1905, Admiral Rojestvensky made a dash for Vladivostok through the Tsu channel, the southern entrance to the Sea of Japan. Togo intercepted him, and a battle followed which, in its results, stands unique in the history of naval warfare. At a cost of three torpedo boats, 113 killed, and 444 wounded, the Japanese sank 6 Russian battleships, 1 coast defense vessel, 3 special service boats, and 3 destroyers, besides capturing 2 battleships, 2 coast defense vessels, and 1 destroyer, The losses in killed were 8,550 and over 3,000 prisoners, among them Admirals Rojestvensky and Nebogatoff, were taken to Japan. As a result of this one-sided battle, Russia's naval power is broken. (May 27-28, 1905.)

While President Theodore Roosevelt seized this opportunity to approach the belligerents in favor of peace, pointing out the hopelessness of continuing the struggle to Russia and appealing to Japan's magnanimity, the world was startled by the revolt of the Kniaz Potemkin, a first-class battleship of the Black Sea squadron. The mutineers found no support, and what might have proved a serious danger to the house of Romanoff, ended by the ship being sunk in Roumanian waters. She was recovered by the Russians.

President Roosevelt's efforts toward bringing the two powers together, proved successful. Washington was agreed upon as the place for the negotiations, but the plenipotentiaries, Sergius Witte and Baron de Rosen acting for Russia, met Baron Komura and Minister Takahira, who represented Japan, at Portsmouth, N. H., where the United States acted as host.

The incompatibility of Japan's demands and Russia's concessions on several occasions brought the plenipotentiaries on the verge of rupture. With the single-mindedness born of an unselfish purpose, President Roosevelt exerted all the personal influence he could bring to bear upon czar and emperor with the result that the victor gave the world an astounding lesson in magnanimity. Japan made peace possible by withdrawing her demands for indemnity and the cession of territory beyond that of which Russia had robbed her,—the southern half of the island of Sakhalin, which will be once more Karafuto for the Japanese.

The terms of the Treaty of Peace were agreed upon at Portsmouth on the 29th of August 1905. The war had lasted from the 5th of February, 1904, or 572 days. Russia paid in men 375,000, in money $1,075,000,000,—all for peaceful absorption and support of prestige. Cassini's shrewd move, ten years before, in robbing Japan of the Liaotung Peninsula and Port Arthur, has ended in Japan's obtaining possession of that key to Peking, with the promise of holding it beyond the possibility of recapture, until China recovers its manhood. The Treaty of Peace was signed September 5, at Portsmouth, N. H.

What will be the effect of the war upon the Russian people? While the plenipotentiaries were discussing the terms of peace, autocracy launched a ukase calling for a consultative assembly. Russian thinkers, however, reflect that, so long as autocracy exists and the tchinovnik admit no other authority but that of the czar, another ukase may revoke the doubtful boon.

No one knows what the morrow will bring, either to us or to the Slav. Yet it seems absurd to suppose that, after the lessons of corruption and incompetence of the present government, the educated Russians will remain quiescent while the great empire continues on its downward course. Mediaevalism has come into contact with the spirit of the twentieth century, and has been found wanting. It seems as if the dawn of a new era for Russia is at hand.

Choose from Thousands of 1stWorldLibrary Classics By

A. M. Barnard
Ada Leverson
Adolphus William Ward
Aesop
Agatha Christie
Alexander Aaronsohn
Alexander Kielland
Alexandre Dumas
Alfred Gatty
Alfred Ollivant
Alice Duer Miller
Alice Turner Curtis
Alice Dunbar
Allen Chapman
Alleyne Ireland
Ambrose Bierce
Amelia E. Barr
Amory H. Bradford
Andrew Lang
Andrew McFarland Davis
Andy Adams
Angela Brazil
Anna Alice Chapin
Anna Sewell
Annie Besant
Annie Hamilton Donnell
Annie Payson Call
Annie Roe Carr
Annonaymous
Anton Chekhov
Archibald Lee Fletcher
Arnold Bennett
Arthur C. Benson
Arthur Conan Doyle
Arthur M. Winfield
Arthur Ransome
Arthur Schnitzler
Arthur Train
Atticus
B.H. Baden-Powell
B. M. Bower
B. C. Chatterjee
Baroness Emmuska Orczy
Baroness Orczy
Basil King
Bayard Taylor
Ben Macomber
Bertha Muzzy Bower
Bjornstjerne Bjornson

Booth Tarkington
Boyd Cable
Bram Stoker
C. Collodi
C. E. Orr
C. M. Ingleby
Carolyn Wells
Catherine Parr Traill
Charles A. Eastman
Charles Amory Beach
Charles Dickens
Charles Dudley Warner
Charles Farrar Browne
Charles Ives
Charles Kingsley
Charles Klein
Charles Hanson Towne
Charles Lathrop Pack
Charles Romyn Dake
Charles Whibley
Charles Willing Beale
Charlotte M. Braeme
Charlotte M. Yonge
Charlotte Perkins Stetson
Clair W. Hayes
Clarence Day Jr.
Clarence E. Mulford
Clemence Housman
Confucius
Coningsby Dawson
Cornelis DeWitt Wilcox
Cyril Burleigh
D. H. Lawrence
Daniel Defoe
David Garnett
Dinah Craik
Don Carlos Janes
Donald Keyhoe
Dorothy Kilner
Dougan Clark
Douglas Fairbanks
E. Nesbit
E. P. Roe
E. Phillips Oppenheim
E. S. Brooks
Earl Barnes
Edgar Rice Burroughs
Edith Van Dyne
Edith Wharton

Edward Everett Hale
Edward J. O'Biren
Edward S. Ellis
Edwin L. Arnold
Eleanor Atkins
Eleanor Hallowell Abbott
Eliot Gregory
Elizabeth Gaskell
Elizabeth McCracken
Elizabeth Von Arnim
Ellem Key
Emerson Hough
Emilie F. Carlen
Emily Bronte
Emily Dickinson
Enid Bagnold
Enilor Macartney Lane
Erasmus W. Jones
Ernie Howard Pie
Ethel May Dell
Ethel Turner
Ethel Watts Mumford
Eugene Sue
Eugenie Foa
Eugene Wood
Eustace Hale Ball
Evelyn Everett-green
Everard Cotes
F. H. Cheley
F. J. Cross
F. Marion Crawford
Fannie E. Newberry
Federick Austin Ogg
Ferdinand Ossendowski
Fergus Hume
Florence A. Kilpatrick
Fremont B. Deering
Francis Bacon
Francis Darwin
Frances Hodgson Burnett
Frances Parkinson Keyes
Frank Gee Patchin
Frank Harris
Frank Jewett Mather
Frank L. Packard
Frank V. Webster
Frederic Stewart Isham
Frederick Trevor Hill
Frederick Winslow Taylor

Friedrich Kerst
Friedrich Nietzsche
Fyodor Dostoyevsky
G.A. Henty
G.K. Chesterton
Gabrielle E. Jackson
Garrett P. Serviss
Gaston Leroux
George A. Warren
George Ade
Geroge Bernard Shaw
George Cary Eggleston
George Durston
George Ebers
George Eliot
George Gissing
George MacDonald
George Meredith
George Orwell
George Sylvester Viereck
George Tucker
George W. Cable
George Wharton James
Gertrude Atherton
Gordon Casserly
Grace E. King
Grace Gallatin
Grace Greenwood
Grant Allen
Guillermo A. Sherwell
Gulielma Zollinger
Gustav Flaubert
H. A. Cody
H. B. Irving
H.C. Bailey
H. G. Wells
H. H. Munro
H. Irving Hancock
H. R. Naylor
H. Rider Haggard
H. W. C. Davis
Haldeman Julius
Hall Caine
Hamilton Wright Mabie
Hans Christian Andersen
Harold Avery
Harold McGrath
Harriet Beecher Stowe
Harry Castlemon
Harry Coghill
Harry Houidini

Hayden Carruth
Helent Hunt Jackson
Helen Nicolay
Hendrik Conscience
Hendy David Thoreau
Henri Barbusse
Henrik Ibsen
Henry Adams
Henry Ford
Henry Frost
Henry James
Henry Jones Ford
Henry Seton Merriman
Henry W Longfellow
Herbert A. Giles
Herbert Carter
Herbert N. Casson
Herman Hesse
Hildegard G. Frey
Homer
Honore De Balzac
Horace B. Day
Horace Walpole
Horatio Alger Jr.
Howard Pyle
Howard R. Garis
Hugh Lofting
Hugh Walpole
Humphry Ward
Ian Maclaren
Inez Haynes Gillmore
Irving Bacheller
Isabel Cecilia Williams
Isabel Hornibrook
Israel Abrahams
Ivan Turgenev
J.G.Austin
J. Henri Fabre
J. M. Barrie
J. M. Walsh
J. Macdonald Oxley
J. R. Miller
J. S. Fletcher
J. S. Knowles
J. Storer Clouston
J. W. Duffield
Jack London
Jacob Abbott
James Allen
James Andrews
James Baldwin

James Branch Cabell
James DeMille
James Joyce
James Lane Allen
James Lane Allen
James Oliver Curwood
James Oppenheim
James Otis
James R. Driscoll
Jane Abbott
Jane Austen
Jane L. Stewart
Janet Aldridge
Jens Peter Jacobsen
Jerome K. Jerome
Jessie Graham Flower
John Buchan
John Burroughs
John Cournos
John F. Kennedy
John Gay
John Glasworthy
John Habberton
John Joy Bell
John Kendrick Bangs
John Milton
John Philip Sousa
John Taintor Foote
Jonas Lauritz Idemil Lie
Jonathan Swift
Joseph A. Altsheler
Joseph Carey
Joseph Conrad
Joseph E. Badger Jr
Joseph Hergesheimer
Joseph Jacobs
Jules Vernes
Julian Hawthrone
Julie A Lippmann
Justin Huntly McCarthy
Kakuzo Okakura
Karle Wilson Baker
Kate Chopin
Kenneth Grahame
Kenneth McGaffey
Kate Langley Bosher
Kate Langley Bosher
Katherine Cecil Thurston
Katherine Stokes
L. A. Abbot
L. T. Meade

L. Frank Baum
Latta Griswold
Laura Dent Crane
Laura Lee Hope
Laurence Housman
Lawrence Beasley
Leo Tolstoy
Leonid Andreyev
Lewis Carroll
Lewis Sperry Chafer
Lilian Bell
Lloyd Osbourne
Louis Hughes
Louis Joseph Vance
Louis Tracy
Louisa May Alcott
Lucy Fitch Perkins
Lucy Maud Montgomery
Luther Benson
Lydia Miller Middleton
Lyndon Orr
M. Corvus
M. H. Adams
Margaret E. Sangster
Margret Howth
Margaret Vandercook
Margaret W. Hungerford
Margret Penrose
Maria Edgeworth
Maria Thompson Daviess
Mariano Azuela
Marion Polk Angellotti
Mark Overton
Mark Twain
Mary Austin
Mary Catherine Crowley
Mary Cole
Mary Hastings Bradley
Mary Roberts Rinehart
Mary Rowlandson
M. Wollstonecraft Shelley
Maud Lindsay
Max Beerbohm
Myra Kelly
Nathaniel Hawthrone
Nicolo Machiavelli
O. F. Walton
Oscar Wilde

Owen Johnson
P.G. Wodehouse
Paul and Mabel Thorne
Paul G. Tomlinson
Paul Severing
Percy Brebner
Percy Keese Fitzhugh
Peter B. Kyne
Plato
Quincy Allen
R. Derby Holmes
R. L. Stevenson
R. S. Ball
Rabindranath Tagore
Rahul Alvares
Ralph Bonehill
Ralph Henry Barbour
Ralph Victor
Ralph Waldo Emmerson
Rene Descartes
Ray Cummings
Rex Beach
Rex E. Beach
Richard Harding Davis
Richard Jefferies
Richard Le Gallienne
Robert Barr
Robert Frost
Robert Gordon Anderson
Robert L. Drake
Robert Lansing
Robert Lynd
Robert Michael Ballantyne
Robert W. Chambers
Rosa Nouchette Carey
Rudyard Kipling
Saint Augustine
Samuel B. Allison
Samuel Hopkins Adams
Sarah Bernhardt
Sarah C. Hallowell
Selma Lagerlof
Sherwood Anderson
Sigmund Freud
Standish O'Grady
Stanley Weyman
Stella Benson
Stella M. Francis

Stephen Crane
Stewart Edward White
Stijn Streuvels
Swami Abhedananda
Swami Parmananda
T. S. Ackland
T. S. Arthur
The Princess Der Ling
Thomas A. Janvier
Thomas A Kempis
Thomas Anderton
Thomas Bailey Aldrich
Thomas Bulfinch
Thomas De Quincey
Thomas Dixon
Thomas H. Huxley
Thomas Hardy
Thomas More
Thornton W. Burgess
U. S. Grant
Upton Sinclair
Valentine Williams
Various Authors
Vaughan Kester
Victor Appleton
Victor G. Durham
Victoria Cross
Virginia Woolf
Wadsworth Camp
Walter Camp
Walter Scott
Washington Irving
Wilbur Lawton
Wilkie Collins
Willa Cather
Willard F. Baker
William Dean Howells
William le Queux
W. Makepeace Thackeray
William W. Walter
William Shakespeare
Winston Churchill
Yei Theodora Ozaki
Yogi Ramacharaka
Young E. Allison
Zane Grey

www.ingramcontent.com/pod-product-compliance
Lightning Source LLC
Chambersburg PA
CBHW050033180626
46810CB00002B/702